Extending & Embedding Python Using C

Mike James

I/O Press
I Programmer Library

Mike James,
Extending & Embedding Python Using C
ISBN Paperback: 9781871962833
ISBN Hardback: 9781871962123
First Printing, 2023
Revision 0

Published by IO Press   www.iopress.info
In association with I Programmer   www.i-programmer.info
and with I o T Programmer   www.iot-programmer.com

The publisher recognizes and respects all marks used by companies and manufacturers as a means to distinguish their products. All brand names and product names mentioned in this book are trade marks or service marks of their respective companies and our omission of trade marks is not an attempt to infringe on the property of others.

For updates, errata, links to resources and the source code for the programs in this book, visit its dedicated page on the IO Press website: iopress.info.

Preface

Writing a C extension for Python is good for fun and profit! The fun part is that adding Python to C gives you so much more power and a deeper understanding of how Python works. The internals of Python are worth knowing about because they suggest new approaches to other problems. As well as being interesting, it is also a valuable skill. The C API, which is what you use to create an extension, is essentially the Python runtime and so exploring it tells you a lot about Python.

You don't need to be an expert Python programmer to create an extension, but it helps. As you are going to be writing mostly C code, programming in C is a more important skill for this task. You don't have to be a C expert, but you do need to be reasonably competent and C aficionados will quickly find out about some of the clever techniques in use in the C API.

Extending Python is a way of bringing any C-based application or library to a much wider audience. Converting Python functions into C functions is also a way of speeding things up. Moreover, you can provide access to hardware or system features that are usually inaccessible by creating an extension. These ideas are expanded on in the first chapter which also introduces the way in which the Python system is composed of three parts – a compiler that produces bytecode, a virtual machine the Python Virtual Machine (PVM) that obeys the bytecode, and a runtime library.

Next come two chapters on how to get started with development under Linux and Windows, respectively. Both chapters use VS Code as the IDE. However while this is recommended as a way of increasing your efficiency, you can use whatever development environment you are familiar with.

Chapter 4 at is where we start creating extensions with the API and PyObject starting with a "Hello World" example. We also create a Python extension to compute Pi which serves to demonstrate how much faster this is than pure Python.

Chapters 5 and 6 deal with the basics of constructing extension functions – how to convert between Python and C data types and vice versa. Data conversion is one of the most common tasks in using the C API and it goes far beyond handling function arguments and return values.

Chapter 7 starts the examination of Python objects with how to add and work with attributes then Chapter 8 extends this to working with more complex built-in objects such as lists, tuples, slices and dictionaries.

Chapter 9 is about error handling and exceptions and how to check that reference counting is implemented correctly, something that isn't often discussed.

Chapter 10 looks at bytes and strings, including exactly how Python stores Unicode, while Chapter 11 starts our look at adding more complicated data types to modules including completely new types in Chapter 12.

Creating a new class brings with it some additional complications, in particular how to handle garbage collection and inheritance, which is tackled in Chapter 13.

Chapter 14 explains how you have to be aware of the action of the GIL and how to make use of threads in both Python and C to improve the efficiency of your code.

The final chapter explains how to convert the skills you have gained in creating a Python extension to embed Python in a C program. This is a less common requirement, but it has some interesting advantages and possibilities and once you know how to create a Python extension it is easy.

Thanks to my tireless editors Sue Gee and Kay Ewbank. Programming is the art of great precision, but English doesn't come with a built-in linter. Errors that remain, and I hope they are few, are mine.

For the source code for the programs in this book, together with any updates or errata, links to resources etc, visit its dedicated page on the IO Press website: iopress.info.

You can also contact me at mike.james@i-programmer.info

Mike James
September, 2023

Table of Contents

Chapter 15
Embedding Python   **243**

Chapter 1

Extending And Embedding Python

Python is an amazing language. Not only is it beautiful on the outside, its inner workings are quite remarkable as well. Python is implemented in C and its approach to object-oriented computing is easy to understand and also easy to extend and make use of in novel ways. Python is written in C and this makes it very easy to integrate with new C code, which can either extend its functionality or embed it in an another C program. In particular, if you have some C code already written then adding it to Python is an easy way to make it more widely available. It is often said that one reason for the success of Python is that it was possible to use existing C libraries with it without having to rewrite everything. This is possibly an exaggeration as Python has other good qualities, but it certainly helped.

In this book we look at how to add C code to Python so that it can be called from a Python program. This is usually is referred to as extending Python although you could see it just as correctly as extending C!

Why would you want to do this? The reasons are many and various, but one of the most common is to speed things up. A CPU-bound C task can be 50 to 100 times faster than the same task programmed in Python. In addition you can make use of multiple cores to run tasks in parallel and so avoid the restrictions of Python's Global Interpreter Lock (GIL) which only allows a single thread to be active in a Python program. Even though there are moves to remove the GIL from future versions of Python, this is something that isn't going away very soon.

More general reasons for writing an extension is to allow Python programmers access to hardware features or implementations of algorithms that would be just too time-consuming or too inefficient to create in Python. At the extreme you can think of this as making Python into a DSL (Domain Specific Language) suitable for tackling specific programming tasks. For example, NumPy is a Python extension that provides advanced numerical operations.

A less common way of using Python with C is to integrate the Python system with your own standalone C program. This is generally called embedding and it is your C program which has to deal with the user interaction. Often this is done to provide a scripting facility in some application. To allow the Python script to interact with your program you generally have to extend the Python system and so the techniques of writing a C extension apply to embedding too and they can usefully be covered in a single treatment. It is also better to learn all about extending and then add on embedding and hence the first chapters of this book are about extending and the final chapter covers the extras you need to use the same information to embed Python.

CPython

Python is a single language with a number of slightly varying implementations. When most people say Python they mean CPython. This is the standard Python system and it is the reference by which others are judged. There is no abstract specification of the Python language, although creating one has been proposed as a project a number of times. In practice CPython is essentially the language standard and if other implementations do thing differently they have a bug unless there is some good reason.

CPython is the only implementation that this book deals with and it is the only implementation that works in the way described. That is, you can't use the techniques described here to implement extensions in other distributions of Python.

This said, CPython is by far the most used implementation of Python and is the standard.

How Much Python Do I Need To Know?

This is a book about extending Python yet in most cases you don't need to know very much Python to make sense of it. You do not have to be a Python expert. However, to understand what is going on in the C extension code you do need to have an idea of how Python objects work. You need to know about classes and how to use them to create instances. You also need to know about Python's inheritance mechanisms – the way that a class provides shared resources and instances customize and add to those resources. Specifically you need to know about new and init and how to make use of self in method definitions. Understanding how attributes can be implemented as get/set properties would also help, as would an understanding of not just inheritance but how Python deals with multiple inheritance.

None of this is essential if you are prepared to allow for how C extensions do these things, but you will not see how what the C extension does is the same as what the Python feature does.

If you want to know more about Python before moving on then see the first of my earlier books, *Programmer's Python: Everything is an Object*, ISBN: 9781871962741. While not an absolute beginner's book it does cover everything a programmer needs to know in order to understand what is being explored here.

There are also features in Python that make it possible to use C functions directly without having to write any additional C code. That is, Python has a foreign function facility that allows it to call functions in other languages. This is not covered in this book as it is less powerful than writing an extension. However it can be useful in the early stages of prototyping an extension to see if the effort is worth the payback. If you want to know more about this see *Programmer's Python: Everything is Data*, ISBN: 9781871962757.

In Chapter 13 we look at the challenges of writing multi-threaded extensions. In this case you do need to at least be aware that Python has many options for creating and running threads. For example, it supports promises and these are a very good way to allow a C function to be run asynchronously. If you want to know more about Python's treatment of asynchronous code see *Programmer's Python: Async*, ISBN: 9781871962765.

C - What You Need To Know

There is a sense in which C is the main language in this book – it is the one used to write most of the code. As in the case of Python you do not need to be an expert, but knowing some of the more advanced C idioms will help you follow how the Python system works.

Python's C code makes heavy use of pointers and structs. In particular, it makes use of the fact that a pointer to a struct is a good way to implement "inheritance". The idea is based on the fact that a struct pointer can be set to any area of memory and it will treat that area as if it has the fields it defined. For example:

```
typedef struct{
    int32_t field1;
    int32_t field2;
}myStruct1;

typedef struct{
    char field1[8];
}myStruct2;
```

These two structs take the same eight bytes of memory to store their data. We can use this to change the data types of a block of memory.

For example:

```
void *myMemory=malloc(8);
```

myMemory is just a pointer to a block of 8 bytes of memory. If we cast them to struct1 we can treat this as two 32-bit ints:

```
myStruct1 *twoInts= (myStruct1*) myMemory;
twoInts->field1=0x42424242;
twoInts->field2=0x43434343;
```

In exactly the same way, we can treat the same block of memory as eight chars:

```
myStruct2 *chars8=(myStruct2*) myMemory;
chars8[0]="A";
```

A full program demonstrating these ideas is:

```
#include <stdlib.h>
#include <stdio.h>
#include <stdint.h>

typedef struct
{
    int32_t field1;
    int32_t field2;
} myStruct1;

typedef struct
{
    char field1[8];
} myStruct2;

int main()
{
    printf("hello world \n");
    void *myMemory = malloc(8);
    myStruct1 *twoInts = (myStruct1 *)myMemory;
    twoInts->field1 = 0x42424242;
    twoInts->field2 = 0x43434343;
    printf("%d,%d \n", twoInts->field1, twoInts->field2);
    myStruct2 *chars8 = (myStruct2 *)myMemory;
    fwrite(chars8, 1, 8, stdout);
    return 0;
}
```

If you run this program, see the next two chapters for help in setting up a development environment, then you will see the same data presented in two different interpretations.

This technique is often called "type punning" and in the form described above it isn't particularly safe. The problem is that it depends on the exact representation of the data and this is system-dependent. Indeed, in C99 and later, type punning leads to undefined behavior which is to be avoided. The correct way to do the same job is to use a union which behaves in roughly the same way but isn't quite as direct.

Fortunately Python makes use of the same idea of having different struct pointers reference the same block of memory, but with one additional detail. Python always uses type puns which are either an extension or a restriction of one another, for example:

```
typedef struct
{
    int32_t field1;
} myStruct1;

typedef struct
{
    int32_t field1;
    int32_t field2;
} myStruct2;
```

In this case myStruct2 is an extension of myStruct1. Both structs will agree on the first field no matter how the struct is laid out in memory and only myStruct2 cares about how field2 is laid out. They can both be used to reference the same block of memory as long as it is large enough to accommodate myStruct2.

```
void *myMemory=malloc(8);
```

```
myStruct1 *oneInt= (myStruct1*) myMemory;
myStruct2 *twoInt= (myStruct1*) myMemory;
oneInt->field1=0x42;
twoInts->field2=0x43;
```

This sort of type punning is safe. The Python system uses this idea of extending structs repeatedly and it is the general principle behind Python objects and inheritance.

If you view a struct as a way of assigning a set of data types to a block of memory then you should find this easy and it is the only slightly advanced C concept used in the CPython implementation of Python. If you want to know more, see Type Punning in Chapter 10 of Fundamental C: Getting Closer To The Machine by Harry Fairhead, ISBN: 9781871962604.

The Structure Of Python

The Python C API is what you use to extend Python, but what is it and what relationship does it have to the full Python system? To understand this we need to look first at how Python is implemented.

The Python system is composed of three parts – a compiler that produces bytecode, a virtual machine the Python Virtual Machine (PVM) that obeys the bytecode, and a runtime library.

The Python compiler takes a Python program and converts it into bytecode. The bytecode is a low level language that can be thought of as a reduction of the full human readable Python to a more efficient and more primitive form. You might write:

```
num1=1
myanswer=num1+42
```

and the compiler converts this into bytecode which is the equivalent of:

```
4           2 LOAD_CONST          1 (1)
            4 STORE_FAST          0 (num1)

5           6 LOAD_FAST           0 (num1)
            8 LOAD_CONST          2 (42)
           10 BINARY_OP           0 (+)
           14 STORE_FAST          1 (myanswer)
```

You can see that the bytecode breaks the task down into smaller steps. These steps are small enough for the virtual machine, the PVM, to be able to implemented them as calls to functions in the Python runtime. For example, the bytecode is transformed into a single function call:

```
myanswer=PyNumber_Add(num1,const42);
```

The C function PyNumber_Add is responsible for doing the actual addition and returning the result to store in myanswer.

PyNumber_Add is a function in the Python runtime and the PVM uses the runtime to implement almost everything that the bytecode specifies. In this sense, a Python program is reduced to a sequence of calls into the runtime.

The runtime functions are the basis of the C API and it is in this sense that learning how to use the C API gives you insights into how Python works. The compiler and the PVM are fairly standard components of any language implemented in this way, but the runtime very much embodies the design decisions made in creating the language. It is the runtime that supports the features that the language presents to its users.

The Python C API

The Python C API is roughly speaking a subset of the Python runtime. The reason it is a subset is that, once specified as part of the C API, a function cannot be changed without breaking existing extensions. The functions that are exposed in the C API are protected from breaking changes in decimal point upgrades to Python. This is more a hope rather a hard and fast rule as often it is difficult to be sure that a change will not invalidate the source code. In most cases upgrades add functions to the API rather than remove them.

Notice that functions with names that start with an underscore might be accessible from the C API but they are considered private and subject to change at any time.

It is also the case that decimal point upgrades to Python do not generally require a recompile of your extension – they are binary compatible. However, the same is not true for larger version increments. That is, you will have to compile your extension for Python 3.9 and Python 3.10.

Python 3.2 introduced a tighter specification for the C API, the Limited API, which is stable across all Python decimal point versions with both source code and binary compatibility. What this means is that if you can restrict yourself to the Limited API you can expect your extensions to work without having to be recompiled across all Python versions 3.x.

To restrict yourself to the Limited API define:

```
Py_LIMITED_API
```

to the lowest version you want to support. In practice, this is not only limiting, it is sometimes slower as the limited API enhances functions so that they support older versions which, often is slower than using the modern optimized function. In most cases it is better to develop your extension using the full C API and see if you need functions outside of the Limited API. All of the code in the following chapters uses the full C API.

Just Enough Simplicity

The examples in this book follow the principle of "just enough simplicity". They do the job intended, but they may not do it in the most compact way and they mostly ignore error handling. The reason is that the purpose of the examples is not to create production quality code, but to explain the ideas clearly enough so that you can create production quality code. For the same reason many of the examples are not practical in the sense that they don't do anything that you would actually want to do. This is much like the principle of "Hello World" – is this a useful program? The answer is yes, but only as an example.

For the same reason all of the programs are in C rather than C++. If you want to use C++ then all you need to do is know how to use it to call the C functions that the API is based on. The examples in this book would gain nothing from being infiltrated by C++.

What all of this means is that after you have understood the examples and what they tell you about using the C API, it is up to you to add error handling and write something useful,! perhaps using C++.

A Route Map

It is always a good idea to know where you are going and so it is with a book. The next two chapters explain how to get started with development under Linux and Windows. Both chapters use VS Code as the IDE, but, while this is recommended as a way of increasing your efficiency, you can use whatever development environment you are familiar with.

It is worth noting at this stage that, while Linux development is based on the well-known GCC compiler, Windows development makes use of the Microsoft C++ compiler as a C compiler. This is unusual as most Windows C programmers opt to install the GCC compilers, even though this isn't easy and not native Windows. However, Python itself uses the Microsoft C compiler but, while you could build extensions using GCC under Windows, it is simpler to stick with the Microsoft compiler and Chapter 3 explains how.

Once we have a development environment setup our first exercise is to create the simplest extension we can – a "Hello World" extension in Chapter 4. To demonstrate that we can do something useful the chapter closes with a look at how to compute Pi and how much faster this is than pure C. Chapters 5 and 6 deal with the basics of constructing extension functions – how to convert between Python and C data types and vice versa. Data conversion is one of the most common tasks in using the C API and it goes far beyond handling function arguments and return values.

Chapter 7 starts the examination of Python objects with how to add and work with attributes. Chapter 8 extends this to working with more complex built-in objects, lists, tuples, slices and dictionaries. Although the Python str is just a list with a specific type of item and some additional methods its use of Unicode is central to the way Python deals with text and this is the subject of Chapter 9. Not only do we have to understand the idea of encoding but exactly how Python stores Unicode.

Chapter 10 starts our look at adding more complicated data types to modules including completely new types in Chapter 11. Creating a new type or class is often the main goal of an extension and this is in many ways the high point in learning to work with the C API. However creating a new class brings with it some additional complications in particular how to handle garbage collection and inheritance which is the subject of Chapter 12.

Chapter 13 explains how you have to be aware of the action of the GIL and how to make use of threads in both Python and C to improve the efficiency of your code. It also deals with the almost legacy topic of implementing callbacks.

The final chapter assumes everything described earlier and makes use of it to embed Python in a C program. To do this you have to modify how you compile the program and generally find out how to interact with the compiler and the PVM.

Summary

- Creating a Python extension in C is not only practically useful it also extends your understanding of the complete Python system.

- You don't need to know much Python to achieve this but you do need to be fairly good at C programming – after all it is mostly C code you are creating.

- The Python system is based on three general components – the compiler, the PVM virtual machine and the runtime library.

- The runtime library is the basis of the C API which is used to extend Python. Essentially your C program calls the Python runtime just as the Python program does.

- The Python C API is relatively stable subset of the runtime but unless you restrict yourself to a limited subset you will have to compile it for each version of Python you are going to support.

- Examples in this book are just that – examples. They usually lack error handling and other niceties. They are not production ready code but once you have the general idea of how things work it will be easy to create production quality code.

- All of the examples in this book aim for simplicity of explanation.

Chapter 2

A First C Module Using Linux

Starting to create Python extensions can be challenging. Once you have your first, even trivial, extension up and running then you can make steady progress to your finished product. Getting started however has a high barrier and none of the existing documentation is particularly helpful. It all looks easy until you actually try it and then the range of things that can go wrong with the configuration is very wide and very difficult to troubleshoot.

In this chapter we concentrate on getting a Linux-based development system up and running. This is in general an easier task than getting a Windows-based development system up and running and, if you can, it is worth starting with Linux, even if your final target is Windows. In practice, you generally want to develop an extension for both Windows and Linux to allow as many people as possible to make use of it.

If you have a choice start with Linux.

You can develop extensions using nothing but the command line, but it is much easier to use an IDE or a code editor. If you are an experienced C programmer you probably have your own preferences and a development environment already set up. In this case you can easily adapt the instructions given in this chapter to your own setup simply by considering what compiler options and settings are in use.

There are Python modules designed for creating extensions and packaging them. The best known, and the one most prominent in the documentation, is distutils. This is is deprecated, to be removed in Python 3.12. Its functionality for specifying package builds is replaced by third-party packages, setup tools and packaging, For reasons of simplicity and clarity these packages are not used in this book. If you need to create a Python package you might find setup tools useful.

In the rest of this chapter, and throughout this book, Visual Studio Code (VS Code) is used as the development environment. The reason for this is that it is open source, relatively easy to use and supports a range of languages including C and Python. To make the procedure as foolproof as possible we'll first check that it is possible to compile a simple C program and then move on to compiling and using a simple extension.

For simplicity the basic C/C++ VS Code extension is used to compile the test extension. For a real project you are most likely going to need to use a make system. VS Code has good support for CMake and this or Make is what you can use to to work with multi-file projects. For simplicity, the examples do not use CMake or Make as they are all single file projects.

GCC and VS Code

The recommended compiler for Python extensions under Linux is the latest version of GCC. If you are using Linux you should have the GCC compiler already installed. You can check this by entering:

```
gcc —version
```

at the command line.

If you don't see a response either you don't have GCC installed or it is missing from the PATH. Installing GCC on Linux is usually easy. For example, under Debian-derived systems use:

```
sudo apt-get install build-essential gdb
```

This installs both GCC and the GDB debugger.

Once you have checked that you have GCC installed you can move on to installing VS Code. As its installation procedure changes very frequently, the best advice is to follow the current instructions on the website:

```
https://code.visualstudio.com/.
```

Install accepting all the defaults unless you know better.

Once you have VS Code installed you need to add the three C/C++ extensions:

If you install the C/C++ extension you will be offered the other two as suggestions and if you install the Extension Pack you get CMake and CMake Tools automatically. CMake is the best way to keep control of a large multi-file project but you don't need it for small single-file examples such as Hello World. If VS Code offers to configure CMake for you, select the option to ignore CMake.

Before moving on to a Hello World example it is worth checking that VS Code can find GCC. Using the VS Code terminal enter:

```
gcc –version
gdb –version
```

If either don't work check your machine's path environment variable or reinstall the package.

Hello World

To create a simple example, first select the File Explorer and click the Open Folder button, navigate to a suitable location and, using right-click and New, create a new folder called CProjects and open it. Create another folder called HelloWorld inside it. You don't have to organize your projects in this way, but it is easier if each C program has its own folder within a top-level workspace folder:

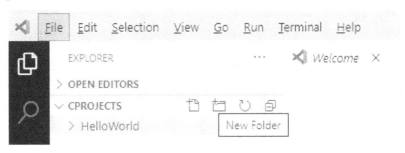

Finally create a file called hello.c in the HelloWorld folder and enter:

```c
#include <stdio.h>
int main(int argc, char **argv)
{
        printf("Hello C World\n");
        return 0;
}
```

You can compile and run the program by selecting the Run icon in the left hand panel and then selecting the compiler you want to use:

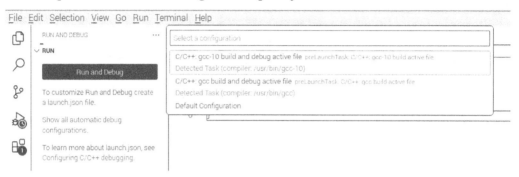

The program should be compiled and you will see the message displayed in the terminal window.

After this VS Code will use the details that it has stored in the `tasks.json` file to implement the build. If things go wrong just delete the file and try running the program again and VS Code will regenerate it for you. `tasks.json` is an important file because it is where you can specify the command line parameters that are passed to the compiler and the linker and these are instrumental in making the change from building a simple command line program to building a Python extension.

Building a Python Extension

Now that we have checked that VS Code and GCC are working it is time to move on to build a Python extension. Rather than spending time explaining how a Python extension works we will use a very basic "hello world extension" program which simply adds two numbers together and returns the result. Exactly how this extension works is explained in Chapter 4. For the moment we simply use it as a proof that our build process works.

Open a new folder called `arithmodule` and create a file called `arith.c` containing the code listed below. The names you give the folder and the file are fairly irrelevant, but it helps to keep it meaningful. You can type the code in as listed or you can copy and paste from the book's webpage at `www.iopress.info`:

```
#define PY_SSIZE_T_CLEAN
#include <Python.h>

static PyObject * add(PyObject *self, PyObject *args)
{
 int x, y, sts;
 if (!PyArg_ParseTuple(args, "ii", &x, &y))
     return NULL;
 sts = x+y;
 return PyLong_FromLong(sts);
}

static PyMethodDef AddMethods[] = {
 {"add", add, METH_VARARGS, "add two numbers"},
 {NULL, NULL, 0, NULL} // sentinel
};

static struct PyModuleDef addmodule = {
 PyModuleDef_HEAD_INIT,
 "arith",
 "C library for sum",
  -1,
  AddMethods
};

PyMODINIT_FUNC PyInit_arith(void) {
     return PyModule_Create(&addmodule);
}
```

This creates an extension that has a single function sum(x,y) which returns the sum of x and y. The code sets the module name to arith and the name of the function to sum. Notice that it is the code that determines these names, not the names of the folders and files used for the project.

The first problem we have is that we need to include the header file Python.h and this isn't stored on the standard header file path. With VS Code there are generally two ways to set an include path – one for the compiler and one for Intellisense. If you set the correct paths for the compiler the code will compile and hopefully work but Intellisense will still show nonexistent errors in the editors if it can't find the include files. Ideally you need to set both, but only the compiler is essential.

Most versions of Linux will have Python and the development libraries already installed. To make sure that the development libraries are installed use:

```
sudo apt-get install python-dev
```

or

```
sudo apt-get install pythonx.y-dev
```

where x and y are the major and minor Python version numbers.

To set the include file for the compiler we have to edit the `tasks.json` file to indicate where the header is stored. In most cases this is:

`usr/include/pythonxy`

where x and y are the major and minor Python version numbers. You can set the location of the include files using an environment variable, but it is simpler and more direct to add it as an option to the GCC compiler in `tasks.json`:

`"-I/usr/include/python3.9",`

To generate a shared library `.so` file we also need to add

`-shared`

and change the name of the file to `arith.so`.

The complete `tasks.json` is:

```
{
    "tasks": [
        {
            "type": "cppbuild",
            "label": "C/C++: gcc-10 build active file",
            "command": "/usr/bin/gcc-10",
            "args": [
                "-fdiagnostics-color=always",
                "-g",
                "-shared",
                "${file}",
                "-o",
                "arith.so",
                "-I/usr/local/include/python3.11"
            ],
            "options": {
                "cwd": "${fileDirname}"
            },
            "problemMatcher": [
                "$gcc"
            ],
            "group": {
                "kind": "build",
                "isDefault": true
            },
            "detail": "Task generated by Debugger."
        }
    ],
    "version": "2.0.0"
}
```

The command line that this generates to build the library is:

```
/usr/bin/gcc-10 -fdiagnostics-color=always -g -shared
  /home/mike/Documents/PExpansion/Arith/arithmodule.c
    -o arith.so -I/usr/include/python3.9
```

This works and finds the necessary include file. You don't need to specify the location of the Python shared library to link to because it is stored in one of the standard system directories. If for any reason the linker cannot find the library you need to locate:

```
libpythonx.y.so
```

where x and y are the major and minor version numbers. Once you have the libraries location you can add:

```
-lpath/libpythonx.y.so
```

to the `args` section of `task.json`.

This should now all work but the Intellisense prompting will still be showing an error in the editor. The solution to this is to add the line:

```
"/usr/include/**"
```

to the include path in `c_cpp_properties.json` giving:

```
{
    "configurations": [
        {
            "name": "Linux",
            "includePath": [
                "${workspaceFolder}/**",
                "/usr/include/**"

            ],
            "defines": [],
            "compilerPath": "/usr/bin/gcc",
            "cStandard": "c17",
            "cppStandard": "gnu++14",
            "intelliSenseMode": "linux-gcc-arm"
        }
    ],
    "version": 4
}
```

Now not only should the program compile, it should also show no errors in the editor. The best way to compile it is to use `Terminal, Run Build Task` as this doesn't attempt to start or debug an executable. After the build you should find `arith.so` in the same folder as the program.

Testing the Module

The final check is to make sure that the new module can be used within a Python program. You can do this in VS Code.

To make running Python programs easy you first need to install the Microsoft Python extension which automatically installs Pylance:

Now you can add a new file to the project called `test.py` with the code:

```
import arith
print(arith.add(1,2))
print(dir(arith))
```

As the current project folder isn't on the Python import path, Pylance will mark the import as an error. To put the current folder on the import path we need to use the extension settings command. Use the command `File`, `Settings` and then select Pylance in the list of extensions. You need to add the `workspaceFolder` to the `Anaylsis:include` setting:

If you do this then the Pylance error on the import statement will vanish.

When you run the program you should see:

```
3
['__doc__', '__file__', '__loader__', '__name__',
                    '__package__', '__spec__', 'add']
```

Notice that the function has the standard methods as well as the custom add function.

Getting the Latest Python

Linux distributions vary in how up-to-date their standard version of Python is. If you are developing an extension then it makes sense to work with the latest stable version of Python. If you have already got GCC installed and working then the effort to download and compile the latest Linux is small.

If you want to make use of the Python debugger you need to make sure that `libffi-dev` is installed:

```
sudo apt-get install libffi-dev
```

As long as it is, Python will be compiled to support the debugger. The next step is to download the source code from the Python website and uncompress it. It doesn't matter where you extract it to as you are going to use it to compile the Python system and after that you can delete it.

Once you have changed directory to the uncompressed source files you simply use the commands:

```
./configure --enable-optimizations
sudo make altinstall
```

The first takes a few minutes and the second tens of minutes. Any errors usually relate to missing dependencies and to fix them all you have to do is install the missing components and recompile.

In most cases your new version of Python will be installed in `usr\local` in the `bin`, `include` and `lib` subdirectories.

To make sure that you get the latest version of Python when you run something from the command line you will usually have to update a link stored in `usr/local/bin`, for example:

```
sudo rm python
sudo ln -s /usr/local/bin/python3.10 python
```

Check that this has worked using:

```
python —version.
```

If you are using VS Code then you can set the Python interpreter to use without having to reconfigure the system. All you have to do is click on the Python version displayed in the bottom right and set the path to the interpreter:

After this VS Code will use the new version of Python by default.

Multimodal Debugging

This is an advanced topic and you can skip it and come back to it when you need to debug an extension – you will need to find out how run a debugger on an extension at some point. Of course, the problem is that there are two programming languages involved – Python and C. We need to use two debuggers we need multimodal debugging.

The Python debugger can be invoked in the usual way when the Python program is run, but the C debugger can only be invoked when our C program is doing something. It has to be attached to the Python system running in response to starting the Python program. Of course, we can't attach the C debugger until the Python program is running and, if we just let the Python program run, it will end before we have a chance to attach the debugger. The solution is that we have to pause the Python program while it is debugging, then start the C debugger and finally start the Python program again.

We need to set up VS Code with two debugging profiles. Using the standard gdb debugger the launch.json file is:

```json
{
    "version": "0.2.0",
    "configurations": [
      {
          "name": "Python: Current File",
          "type": "python",
          "request": "launch",
          "program": "${file}",
          "console": "integratedTerminal"
      },
      {
          "name": "(gdb) Attach",
          "type": "cppdbg",
          "request": "attach",
          "program": "/usr/local/bin/python3.11",
          "processId": "${command:pickProcess}",
          "MIMode": "gdb",
          "setupCommands": [
              {
                  "description": "Enable pretty-printing for gdb",
                  "text": "-enable-pretty-printing",
                  "ignoreFailures": true
              }
          ]
      }
    ]
}
```

You have to change "`program`": to be the path to the Python interpreter. The big problem is that you have to set the `processId` of the Python process and this isn't something you can know or set in advance. The solution is that the `pickProcess` command gives you a drop-down list from which you can select the process and this is not always easy.

With this `launch.json` the procedure to debug an extension is:

1. Put a breakpoint in the Python program just before the code in your extension that is to be executed – it can be in the statement that imports it.

2. Start the Python program running in debug mode and wait for it to stop on the breakpoint.

3. Put a breakpoint in the C program where you want it to stop – it has to be somewhere that the Python program will call into.

4. Go to the Run and Debug view and select gdb Attach, click the run button:

5. You will next be asked to select the process to attach to. Type P and you will see just the Python programs running:

The one that you want to attach to is the one with the adapter access token and you should select it – it is usually the last one in the list.

6. Now single-step through the Python program so that it calls your extension.

7. This should cause the C program to pause at the breakpoint – as long as the Python program calls the code that contains the breakpoint.

You can now use the debugger to step through the code of both programs. Initially it can be difficult to work out how to get to a particular section of the C code, but you quickly get used to it. The only frustrating part is having to repeatedly specify the process Id for the Python program.

Notice that if everything is set up correctly you should be able to single-step and examine calls into the C API.

Summary

- Linux is an easy-to-use development system because it generally is preconfigured with the GCC compiler and gdb debugger.

- Although you can use the command line or any IDE, there are advantages in using VS Code as it is open source and supports both Python and C.

- It is worth checking that everything is installed correctly by creating a Hello World program.

- To build a Python extension you have to specify both the include directory and that a shared `.so` library is to be generated.

- To make the Intellisense prompting work correctly you have to define a `c_cpp_properties.json` file.

- Testing an extension is a matter of running a Python program that imports it and then makes use of it.

- As you have GCC installed, it is relatively easy to compile the latest version of Python to use.

- At some point you are going to need to work out how to debug an extension. This involves running a debugger for the Python program and a separate debugger for the C program.

Chapter 3

A First C Module Using Windows

Windows is more difficult to get started with than Linux partly because we have to use the Microsoft Visual C++ (MSVC) compiler and this isn't as well-documented for use on the command line as GCC is. You can use GCC under Windows if you want to, but Python under Windows is compiled using MSVC and this is the recommended compiler for extensions.

In the rest of this chapter Visual Studio Code (VS Code) is used as the development environment along with MSVC. The reason for this is that it is open source, relatively easy to use and supports a range of languages including C and Python. To make the procedure as foolproof as possible we first check that it is possible to compile a simple C program and then move on to compiling and using a simple extension.

For this simple example, compiling using the Microsoft C/C++ extension is good enough. For a real multi-file project you can use CMake or something similar. It is also true that Visual Studio is also a good choice for developing Python extensions. Its only disadvantage is that it is not open source.

VS Code and MSVC

The recommended compiler for Python extensions under Windows is the latest version of Microsoft C/C++ MSVC compiler. Unless you have already installed it or are using Visual Studio, it is unlikely to be available on your system and you will have to install it. This involves installing the Desktop development with C++ workload from the Visual Studio webpage, or you could use the complete Visual Studio installation just to get the desktop development system.

To find the tools you will probably have to search All Downloads for Tools for Visual Studio 2022, or whatever the latest version is.

Build Tools for Visual Studio 2022

These Build Tools allow you to build Visual Studio projects from a command-line interface. Supported projects include: ASP.NET, Azure, C++ desktop, ClickOnce, containers, .NET Core, .NET Desktop, Node.js, Office and SharePoint, Python, TypeScript, Unit Tests, UWP, WCF, and Xamarin. Use of this tool requires a valid Visual Studio license.

Are you looking for one of the Visual Studio 2022 long term servicing baselines (LTSCs)? You can find them here.

Download

When the installer has started select `Desktop development with C/C++`. After this has installed you can use the `Developer Command Prompt` to test that the compiler has been installed properly using the command `cl`.

To make VS Code use the compiler you have to start it from the Developer Command Prompt and a fact that isn't clearly made in the documentation is that the version of the compiler that you use depends on which command prompt is active. The compiler comes in versions that run on 32-bit or 64-bit machines to produce 32-bit or 64-bit code. Which compiler VS Code uses depends on the command prompt used to start it:

- `x64 Native Tools` – 64-bit platform, 64-bit code
- `x86 Native Tools` – 32-bit platform, 32-bit code

On a 64-bit machine you want a 64-bit compiler that produces 64-bit code, so the appropriate choice is the `x64 Native Tools` command prompt. This is very important as you need to match the compiler to the version of Python that you are running. If you don't then, even with everything setup correctly, the linker will complain that it can't find the Python library functions.

You can check that you have MSVC installed and accessible by starting the appropriate Native Tools prompt and entering:

`cl`

i.e. C L in lower case. You should see something like:

```
C:\Program Files (x86)\Microsoft Visual Studio\2022\BuildTools>cl
Microsoft (R) C/C++ Optimizing Compiler Version 19.36.32532 for x64
Copyright (C) Microsoft Corporation.  All rights reserved.
```

Once you have checked that you have MSVC installed you can move on to installing VS Code. As this changes very frequently, the best advice is to follow the current instructions on the website:

`https://code.visualstudio.com/`

Install accepting all the defaults unless you know better.

Start the appropriate command prompt, which for a 64-bit Python system is `x64 Native Tool`, and enter `code`. This runs VS Code and from here you can use it as normal. If you want to use MSVC with the correct architecture via VS Code you have to start VS Code from the Native Tool prompt. If you don't start VS Code from the correct Native Tool prompt nothing much will work.

Once you have VS Code installed you need to add the three C/C++ extensions:

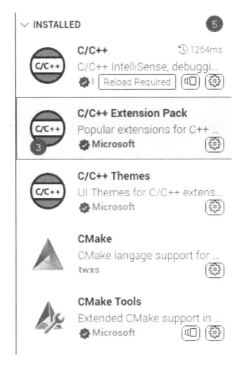

If you install the C/C++ extension you will be offered the other two as suggestions and if you install the Extension Pack you get CMake and CMake Tools automatically. CMake is the best way to keep control of a large multi-file project, but you don't need it for small single-file examples such as Hello World. If VS Code offers to configure CMake for you select the option to ignore CMake.

Before moving on to a Hello World example it is worth checking that VS Code can find MSVC. Using the VS Code terminal enter:

```
cl
```

If it doesn't report the version of the compiler then you have probably not started VS Code from the Native Tool prompt – it is easy to forget!

Hello World

To create a simple example, first select the File Explorer and click the Open Folder button, navigate to a suitable location and, using right-click and New, create a new folder called CProjects and open it. Create another folder called HelloWorld inside it. You don't have to organize your projects in this way, but it is easier if each C program has its own folder within a top-level workspace folder:

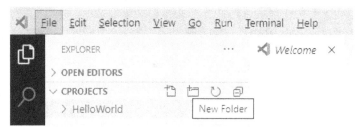

Finally create a file called hello.c in the HelloWorld folder and enter:

```
#include <stdio.h>
int main(int argc, char **argv)
{
        printf("Hello C World\n");
        return 0;
}
```

You can compile and run the program by selecting the Run icon in the left hand panel and then selecting the compiler you want to use C++ (GDB/LLDB):

The program should be compiled and you will see the message displayed in the terminal window.

After this VS Code will use the details that it has stored in the tasks.json file to implement the build. If things go wrong just delete the file and try running the program again and VS Code will regenerate it for you. tasks.json is an important file because it is where you can specify the command line parameters that are passed to the compiler and the linker and these are how we make the change from building a simple command line program to building a Python extension.

Building a Python Extension

Now that we have checked that VS Code and MSVC are working it is time to move on to build a Python extension. Rather than spending time explaining how a Python extension works we will use a very basic "hello extension" program which simply adds two numbers together and returns the result. Exactly how this extension works is explained in Chapter 4. For the moment we simply use it as a proof that our build process works.

Open a new folder called `arithmodule` and create a file called `arith.c` containing the code listed below. The name you give the folder and the file is fairly irrelevant, but it helps to keep it meaningful. You can type the code in as listed or you can copy and paste from the book's webpage at `www.iopress.info`:

```c
#define PY_SSIZE_T_CLEAN
#include <Python.h>

static PyObject * add(PyObject *self, PyObject *args)
{
    int x, y, sts;

    if (!PyArg_ParseTuple(args, "ii", &x, &y))
        return NULL;
    sts = x+y;
    return PyLong_FromLong(sts);
}
static PyMethodDef AddMethods[] = {
    {"add", add, METH_VARARGS, "add two numbers"},
    {NULL, NULL, 0, NULL} // sentinel
};

static struct PyModuleDef addmodule = {
  PyModuleDef_HEAD_INIT,
  "arith",
  "C library for sum",
  -1,
  AddMethods
};

PyMODINIT_FUNC PyInit_arith(void) {
      return PyModule_Create(&addmodule);
}
```

This creates an extension that has a single function `sum(x,y)` which returns the sum of x and y. The code sets the module name to `arith` and the name of the function to sum. Notice that it is the code that determines these names, not the names of the folders and files used for the project.

The first problem we have is that we need to include the header file Python.h and this isn't stored on the standard header file path. With VS Code there are generally two ways to set an include path – one for the compiler and one for Intellisense. If you set the correct paths for the compiler the code will compile and hopefully work, but Intellisense will still show nonexistent errors in the editors if it can't find the include files. Ideally you need to set both, but only the compiler is essential.

If you have installed Python Windows will have the development libraries already installed. Python is installed in either:

C:\Python*xy*

or

C:\Users*username*\AppData\Local\Programs\Python\Python*xy*

where x and y are the major and minor version numbers.

To set the include file for the compiler we have to edit the tasks.json file to indicate where the header is stored. You can set the location of the include files using an environment variable but it is simpler and more direct to add it as an option to the MSVC compiler args in tasks.json:

"/IC:/Users/*user*/AppData/Local/Programs/Python/Python311/include",

To generate a DLL shared library we also need to add:

```
"/link /dll /OUT:arith.pyd /LIBPATH:C:/Users/user/AppData/Local/
                    Programs/Python/Python311/libs"
```

Notice that a DLL compiled for use as a module has the extension .pyd and not the default and more usual .dll and so we have to specify this using the /OUT parameter to the linker. We also have to tell the linker where to look for the Python*xy*.dll file to link with the module as this is not stored on any of the usual DLL paths that the linker searches.

The complete tasks.json is:

```
{
    "tasks": [
        {
            "type": "cppbuild",
            "label": "C/C++: cl.exe build active file",
            "command": "cl.exe",
            "args": [
                "/Zi",
                "/EHsc",
                "/nologo",
                "/IC:/Users/user/AppData/Local/Programs/Python/
                                        Python311/include",
                "${file}",
                "/link /dll /OUT:arith.pyd
                        /LIBPATH:C:/Users/user/AppData/
                        Local/Programs/Python/Python311/libs"
            ],
```

```
            "options": {
                "cwd": "${fileDirname}"
            },
            "problemMatcher": [
                "$msCompile"
            ],
            "group": {
                "kind": "build",
                "isDefault": true
            },
            "detail": "Task generated by Debugger."
        }
    ],
    "version": "2.0.0"
}
```

The command line that this generates to build the library is:

```
cl.exe /Zi /EHsc /nologo /IC:/Users/user/AppData/
   Local/Programs/Python/Python311/include
   C:\Users\user\Documents\projects\arith.c
   "/link /dll /OUT:arith.pyd
   /LIBPATH:C:/Users/user/AppData/
           Local/Programs/Python/Python311/libs"
```

This works and finds the necessary include files.

This should now all work but the Intellisense prompting will still be showing an error in the editor. The Intellisense analysis of your code is controlled by the c_cpp_properties.json file. You can add an autogenerated file using the command C/C++: Edit Configurations (UI) from the command palette. To include the Python header you need to add the line:

```
"C:/Users/user/AppData/Local/Programs/Python/Python311/include/"
```

to the include path in c_cpp_properties.json giving:

```
{
    "configurations": [
        {
            "name": "Win32",
            "includePath": [
                "${workspaceFolder}/**",
                "C:/Users/user/AppData/Local/
                    Programs/Python/Python311/include/"
            ],
            "defines": [
                "_DEBUG",
                "UNICODE",
                "_UNICODE"
            ],
```

```
            "windowsSdkVersion": "10.0.22000.0",
            "compilerPath": "cl.exe",
            "cStandard": "c17",
            "cppStandard": "c++17",
            "intelliSenseMode": "windows-msvc-x64"
        }
    ],
    "version": 4
}
```

Now not only should the program compile, it should also show no errors in the editor. The best way to compile it is to use `Terminal, Run Build Task` as this doesn't attempt to start or debug an executable. After the build you should find `arith.pyd` in the same folder as the program.

If you see an error something like:

```
fatal error LNK1112: module machine type 'x64' conflicts...
```

you have started VS Code using the wrong Native Tool prompt.

Testing the Module

The final check is to make sure that the new module can be used within a Python program. You can do this in VS Code.

To make running Python programs easy you first need to install the Microsoft Python extension which automatically installs Pylance:

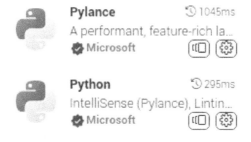

Now you can add a new file to the project called `test.py` with the code:

```
import arith
print(arith.add(1,2))
print(dir(arith))
```

As the current project folder isn't on the Python import path, Pylance will mark the import as an error. To put the current folder on the import path we need to use the extension settings command. Use the command File, Settings and then select Pylance in the list of extensions.

You need to add the `workspaceFolder` to the `Analysis:include` setting:

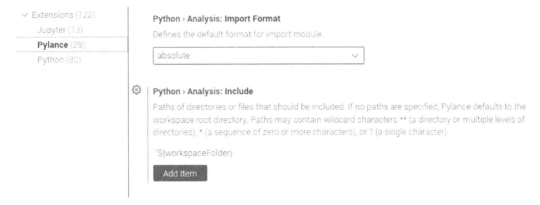

If you do this then the Pylance error on the import statement will vanish.

When you run the program you should see:

```
3
['__doc__', '__file__', '__loader__', '__name__',
                '__package__', '__spec__', 'add']
```

Notice that the function has the standard methods as well as the custom add function.

Multimodal Debugging

This is an advanced topic and you can skip it and come back to it when you need to debug an extension – you will need to find out how run a debugger on an extension at some point. Of course the problem is that there are two programming languages involved – Python and C. We need to use two debuggers we need multimodal debugging.

The Python debugger can be invoked in the usual way when the Python program is run, but the C debugger can only be invoked when our C program is doing something. It has to be attached to the Python system running in response to starting the Python program. Of course, we can't attach the C debugger until the Python program is running and if we just let the Python program run it will end before we have a chance to attach the debugger. The solution is that we have to pause the Python program while it is debugging, then start the C debugger and finally start the Python program again.

We need to set up VS Code up with two debugging profiles. Using the standard Microsoft Visual Studio debugger the `launch.json` file is:

```
{
    "version": "0.2.0",
    "configurations": [
        {
            "name": "(Windows) Attach",
            "type": "cppvsdbg",
            "request": "attach",
            "processId": "${command:pickProcess}",
        },
        {
            "name": "Python: Current File",
            "type": "python",
            "request": "launch",
            "program": "${file}",
            "console": "integratedTerminal"
        }
    ]
}
```

The big problem is that you have to set the `processId` of the Python process and this isn't something you can know or set in advance. The solution is that the `pickProcess` command gives you a drop-down list from which you can select the process and this is not always easy.

With this `launch.json` the procedure to debug an extension is:

1. Put a breakpoint in the Python program just before the code in your extension that is to be executed – it can be in the statement that imports it.

2. Start the Python program running in debug mode and wait for it to stop on the breakpoint.

3. Put a breakpoint in the C program where you want it to stop – it has to be somewhere that the Python program will call for it.

4. Got to the Run and Debug view and select `gdb Attach`, click the green run button:

5. You will next be asked to select the process to attach to. Type P and you will see just the Python programs running:

The one that you want to attach to is the one with the adapter access token and you should select it – its usually the last one in the list.

6. Now single-step through the Python program so that it calls your extension.

7. This should cause the C program to pause at the breakpoint – as long as the Python program calls the code that contains the breakpoint.

You can now use the debugger to step though the code of both programs. Initially it can be difficult to work out how to get to a particular section of the C code but you quickly get used to it. The only frustrating part is having to repeatedly specify the process Id for the Python program.

Notice that if everything is setup correctly you be able to single-step through both your C and Python programs, but not examine calls into the C API.

If you want to debug the Python system as well as your own code you need to install debugging symbols. This can be done during Python installation by ticking the correct boxes:

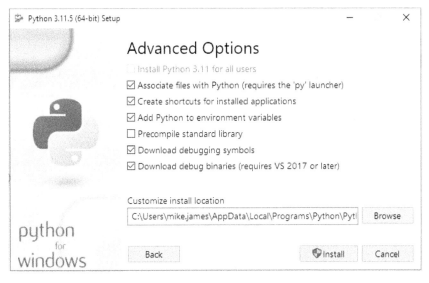

You also need to download the Python source files from the Python website as a Gzipped tarball. You can uncompressed this using 7-Zip or similar to a suitable location. For example, uncompress the complete tarball to the same directory as the compiled Python. It is important that the versions are the same.

To tell VS Code where the source files are you have to add a `sourceFileMap` and a symbol search path to the `launch.json` file:

```
{
    "version": "0.2.0",
    "configurations": [
        {
            "name": "(Windows) Attach",
            "type": "cppvsdbg",
            "request": "attach",
            "processId": "${command:pickProcess}",
            "symbolSearchPath": "C:/Users/user/AppData/Local/
                                  Programs/Python/Python-3.11.4",
            "sourceFileMap":{"D:/a/1/s/":"C:/Users/user/
                            AppData/Local/Programs/Python/Python311"},
        },
        {
            "name": "Python: Current File",
            "type": "python",
            "request": "launch",
            "program": "${file}",
            "console": "integratedTerminal"
        }
    ]
}
```

Of course, you need to modify the path to the source files to be correct for your system.

With this modification you can now single-step and breakpoint within the C API.

Summary

- The Windows development system is slightly harder to use because it doesn't use the GCC and gdb debugger. C programmers are generally less familiar with the Microsoft C compiler and its associated debugger.

- Although you can use the command line or any IDE, there are advantages in using VS Code as it is open source and supports both Python and C.

- It is worth checking that everything is installed correctly by creating a Hello World program.

- To build a Python extension you have to ensure that an include directory has been specified and that a DLL is to be generated. The DLL has the extension .pyd and not the usual .dll.

- To make the Intellisense prompting work correctly you have to define a `c_cpp_properties.json` file.

- Testing an extension is a matter of running a Python program that imports it and then makes use of it.

- At some point you are going to need to work out how to debug an extension. This involves running a debugger for the Python program and a separate debugger for the C program.

- If you want to debug the C API as well as your own code, you need to download a symbols file and the source code and modify the `launch.json` file.

Chapter 4
Module Basics

Now that we know how to build a module, the time has come to discover what goes into coding a module. Mostly this is a matter of making use of the C API and this is the subject of most of this book. There are some basic things that you have to do to make a C program into a module and this is where we start our examination of the API.

The API and PyObject

The Python C API is a collection of functions and "objects" with names that start Py or _Py. The ones named Py form the public API and you can use them. The ones named _Py are supposed to be private and you shouldn't use them.

The most important principle to understand is that everything in Python is represented in the C API as a PyObject – integers, lists, dictionary, functions, everything. The PyObject is a struct that contains very little information about the object – a reference count, see later, and a pointer to a type object which describes the object in question. A PyObject pointer can reference any Python object, but to make use of the object you may have to cast to a more specific type.

The principle is that all Python objects are represented by a specific C struct that is an extension of PyObject and as a result any Python object can be referenced by PyObject*.

The C API contains many of the functions that implement Python. In many cases there is a simple equivalence between Python functions and C functions. For example, the Python function dir(*object*) returns a list of names of the current locals for the specified object. The C API equivalent is pyObject_Dir(PyObject*) which returns a PyObject* pointer to a list of strings corresponding to the locals for the object referenced. The equivalence isn't exact, but if you know your Python you know quite a lot of the C API.

I suppose you could say, in the style of the zen of Python, in the C API everything is a PyObject.

The Initialization Function

An extension module is just a shared library which exports an initialization function which has the signature:

```
PyObject* PyInit_modulename(void)
```

where *modulename* is the ASCII name of the module. If you want to use a Unicode module name you have to use a more complicated initialization called multi-phase initialization, see Chapter 11. When you import a module Python locates the file *modulename*.so under Linux or *modulename*.pyd under Windows and then tries to call `PyInit_modulename`.

This also implies that `PyInit_modulename` is exported from the shared library, i.e. it can be called by an external program. You don't have to do anything to export a function under Linux, but you do need to add __declspec(dllexport) for Windows. The solution is to simply use the PyMODINIT_FUNC macro which will automatically add the necessary __declspec(dllexport) under Windows.

The pointer to PyObject returned should be a fully initialized module as returned by:

```
PyObject* PyModule_Create(PyModuleDef* def)
```

or

```
PyObject *PyModule_Create2(PyModuleDef* def,
                                      int module_api_version)
```

The PyModuleDef struct has fields that determine how the module will be treated by the system:

```
struct PyModuleDef {
  PyModuleDef_Base m_base;
  const char* m_name;
  const char* m_doc;
  Py_ssize_t m_size;
  PyMethodDef *m_methods;
  PyModuleDef_Slot *m_slots;
  traverseproc m_traverse;
  inquiry m_clear;
  freefunc m_free;
};
```

Not all of the fields have to be used. The most important are:

- ◆ `m_base`   always initialize this member to `PyModuleDef_HEAD_INIT`
- ◆ `*m_name`   name of the module
- ◆ `*m_doc`   docstring for the module
- ◆ `m_size`   memory needed to store module state usually -1 for a simple module
- ◆ `*m_methods` pointer to array of `PyMethodDef` structs defines the methods provided by the module

The format of the `PyMethodDef` struct is:

```
struct PyMethodDef {
    const char  *ml_name;
    PyCFunction ml_meth;
    int         ml_flags;
    const char  *ml_doc;
};
```

The fields are:

- ◆ `ml_name`   name of method
- ◆ `ml_meth`   pointer to the function that implements the method
- ◆ `ml_flags` constant indicating how to call the function
- ◆ `ml_doc`   the docstring for the method

The `ml_flags` constant determines the calling convention for the function. For example, if it is set to `METH_VARARGS` then the function is passed two parameters. The first is a `self` which gives the instance if the function is called as a method and the module object if it is called as a function. The second is a tuple holding all of the parameters. Of course, both parameters are `*PyObjects`.

The array of `PyMethodDef` structs is terminated by a sentinel value:

```
{NULL, NULL, 0, NULL}
```

To summarize:

- You have to create an array of `PyMethodDef` specifying the methods/functions that the module provides.

- This is added along with other data to a `PyModuleDef` struct which defines the module.

- The `PyModuleDef` is used in the `PyModule_Create` function to create a module object which is returned by the `PyInit_modulename` function.

Initializing the arith Module

The example of the `arith` module used in the previous chapters is a simple module which provides a single function `add(a,b)` and we can initialize it using the steps just described.

First we need to define the functions and methods it provides:

```
static PyMethodDef AddMethods[] = {
    {"add", add, METH_VARARGS, "add two numbers"},
    {NULL, NULL, 0, NULL} // sentinel
};
```

`PyMethodDef` defines the function that we can call:

```
{"add", add, METH_VARARGS, "add two numbers"}
```

The first field is the name that the Python program uses to call the function and the second is a pointer to the C function that is called. Notice that the two don't have to be the same. For example:

```
{"sum", add, METH_VARARGS, "add two numbers"}
```

would mean that the C function `add` in the module was called when the Python function `sum` was called. The third field `METH_VARARGS` specifies that the parameters are passed as a tuple. The final field is the docstring.

Now that we have the method definitions, we can create the `PyModuleDef` struct:

```
static struct PyModuleDef addmodule = {
  PyModuleDef_HEAD_INIT,
  "arith",
  "C library for sum",
  -1,
  AddMethods
};
```

The name of the module is "arith" and the `AddMethods` struct contains the information about what function are available.

Now all that remains is to write the `add` function so that it can be called by the C API. The only real difference between this and a simple `add` function:

```
int add(int x, int y){
    return x+y;
}
```

is the need to work with `PyObject` as the parameter type and the return type and the need to convert the data from Python format and back to Python format.

```
static PyObject * add(PyObject *self, PyObject *args)
{
    int x, y, sts;
    if (!PyArg_ParseTuple(args, "ii", &x, &y))
        return NULL;
    sts = x+y;
    return PyLong_FromLong(sts);
}
```

The parameters passed to the function are both `PyObjects` – the first is `self`, which in this case is just a pointer to the module object, which is of course just a `PyObject`. The second is a tuple of the parameters passed to the function in Python.

Our next problem is to extract the parameters into data types that C can use. In most cases this is a job for one of the PyArg functions.

```
PyArg_ParseTuple(args, format, variables)
```

will take the tuple pointed at by args and use the specified format to split it into different data types which are stored in the specified variables. This is very similar to the way printf uses a format to print different variables types, although the format codes used are different. In this case, the two arguments are integers and the appropriate format is "ii".

```
PyArg_ParseTuple(args, "ii", &x, &y)
```

stores the two integer arguments in x and y ready for use by the C function. The function returns false if there is an error and returns NULL to signal the error to Python. Once we have the values we can add them and convert them into a form that Python can use via the PyLong_FromLong function.

This is typical. The C function that you want to make available to Python generally needs the Python objects it is passed to be converted to C data types and then any results it produces need to be converted into suitable Python objects.

The complete program has been presented earlier, but it is worth repeating:

```c
#define PY_SSIZE_T_CLEAN
#include <Python.h>

static PyObject * add(PyObject *self, PyObject *args)
{
    int x, y, sts;
    if (!PyArg_ParseTuple(args, "ii", &x, &y))
        return NULL;
    sts = x+y;
    return PyLong_FromLong(sts);
}

static PyMethodDef AddMethods[] = {
    {"add", add, METH_VARARGS, "add two numbers"},
    {NULL, NULL, 0, NULL} // sentinel
};

static struct PyModuleDef addmodule = {
  PyModuleDef_HEAD_INIT,
  "arith",
  "C library for sum",
  -1,
  AddMethods
};

PyMODINIT_FUNC PyInit_arith(void) {
    return PyModule_Create(&addmodule);
}
```

Computing Pi – How Fast?

As a second simple example, we can use a very simple computation to demonstrate the potential speed advantages that a C extension module offers. You can compute pi using the very simple series:

pi = 4*(1-1/3+1/5-1/7 ...)

This is very easy to implement, we just need to generate the odd integers, but to get pi to a reasonable number of digits you have to compute a lot of terms. In other words, this series is very slow to converge. The simple-minded approach is to write something like:

```python
import time
def myPi(m,n):
    pi=0
    for k in range(m,n+1):
        s= 1 if k%2 else -1
        pi += s / (2 * k - 1)
    return 4*pi
```

This computes the sum from m to n.

A main program to make use of this function is:

```python
if __name__ == '__main__':
    N=10000000
    t1=time.perf_counter()
    pi=myPi(1,N)
    t2=time.perf_counter()
    print((t2-t1)*1000)
    print(pi)
```

If you try this out you will find that it gives pi to about five digits, which is not good for so many terms, but it is a good example to convert to a C extension.

The details of initializing the module follow the usual steps and the function is a fairly obvious translation of the Python:

```c
#define PY_SSIZE_T_CLEAN
#include <Python.h>
static PyObject * Pi(PyObject *self, PyObject *args)
{
    int m, n;
    double pi,s;
    if (!PyArg_ParseTuple(args, "ii", &m, &n))
        return NULL;
    pi=0;
    for(int k=m;k<n;k++){
        s=1;
        if(k%2==0)s=-1;
        pi=pi+s/(2*k-1);
    }
    return PyFloat_FromDouble(4*pi);
}
```

```
static PyMethodDef AddMethods[] = {
    {"myPi", Pi, METH_VARARGS, "Compute Pi"},
    {NULL, NULL, 0, NULL} // sentinel
};

static struct PyModuleDef addmodule = {
  PyModuleDef_HEAD_INIT,
  "Pi",
  "C library to compute Pi",
  -1,
  AddMethods
};

PyMODINIT_FUNC PyInit_Pi(void) {
    return PyModule_Create(&addmodule);
}
```

The only real changes are to the names used for the module and function. Task.json also needs to be updated. The args for Windows is:

```
"args": [
                    "/Zi",
                    "/EHsc",
                    "/nologo",
                    "/IC:/Users/user/AppData/Local/Programs
                                        /Python/Python311/include",
                    "${file}",
                    "/link /dll /OUT:Pi.pyd
                        /LIBPATH:C:/Users/user/AppData/Local/
                                        Programs/Python/Python311/libs"
```

For Linux it is:

```
"args": [
                    "-fdiagnostics-color=always",
                    "-g",
                    "-shared",
                    "${file}",
                    "-o",
                    "Pi.so",
                    "-I/usr/include/python311"
```

With these changes the module should compile. If not go back to the instructions in chapters 2 and 3.

A Python program to make use of the module is very similar to the previous program:

```python
import Pi
import time
if __name__ == '__main__':
    N=10000000
    t1=time.perf_counter()
    pi=Pi.myPi(1,N)
    t2=time.perf_counter()
    print((t2-t1)*1000)
    print(pi)
```

So how much faster is the C extension than the pure Python?

The first thing to say is that this extension should exhibit the maximum speed gain. The pure Python program delegates nothing to any existing C modules and the C extension interacts minimally with Python. The only time lost is initializing the module and making the single call to the function. On a middle-of-the range PC the pure Python program takes 2.5 seconds and the extension takes 50ms, a speedup of 50 times. On a Raspberry Pi 4 the pure Python program takes 3.2 seconds and the extension takes 89ms, a speedup of 35 times.

Of course, the speedup you see from using an extension is unlikely to be this great as the task becomes more complex and requires more processing to interface the C and Python code, but it should still be worth the effort.

Example Module

To make the remaining examples easier we can make use of an examples module that you can re-use as a template:

```c
#define PY_SSIZE_T_CLEAN
#include <Python.h>

static PyObject* exampleFunction(PyObject *self, PyObject *args)
{
    //example function code

}

static PyMethodDef AddMethods[] = {
    {"exampleFunction", exampleFunction, METH_VARARGS, "an
example"},
    {NULL, NULL, 0, NULL} // sentinel
};
```

```
static struct PyModuleDef addmodule = {
  PyModuleDef_HEAD_INIT,
  "example",
  "C library to test API",
  -1,
  AddMethods
};

PyMODINIT_FUNC PyInit_example(void) {
    return PyModule_Create(&addmodule);
}
```

Also make sure that the file names used in task.json are correct and that example compiles.

In future chapters we will simply add functions to this module and add them to the method definition. This saves having to repeat the same task.json and launch.json files.

Summary

- The main principle of the C API is that all Python objects are represented by a specific C Struct that is an extension of `PyObject` and as a result any Python object can be referenced by a `PyObject*`

- The C API contains many of the functions that implement Python. In many cases there is a simple equivalence between Python functions and C functions.

- Every module has an initialization function with the name `PyInit_modulename`.

- The initialization function is called when the module is imported and it creates the module object and returns it.

- The `PyModuleDef` struct has fields that determine how the module will be treated by the system.

- An array of `PyMethodDef` structs specifies the methods/functions that the module provides.

- The `PyArg_ParseTuple` function can be used to parse the tuple of arguments passed to the function.

- A simple calculation demonstrates that converting a Python function to C can speed it up by a factor of roughly 50.

- To avoid having to change the compiler settings, a standard example extension is used in the rest of this book.

Chapter 5

Arguments

Many extensions simply provide functions for the Python code to use. In this case the only task that you have is to ensure that the C function can accept the arguments the Python function call passes it and ensure that the C function constructs something meaningful for the Python function to return. The idea is that the C extension will process the Python data faster or in a more sophisticated way than Python could. In most cases this implies that the first task is to convert the Python data to native C data so that the C program can process it as fast as possible. After this fast computation, the task is generally to convert the C data back to a form that Python can make use of. How to build Python objects from C data types is the subject of the next chapter.

What all this means is that in most cases the first task in implementing an extension module is to convert the function's parameters to C data types and the last task is to convert the C data types back to Python data types. This simple picture isn't always accurate as in some cases it is more efficient to work with the Python data in C without any conversion process by calling C API functions and we will look at how to work with Python objects later.

The focus of this chapter is the conversion of Python data to C data. The good news is that the C API provides a good range of functions to perform the conversion of Python and C values. However, the range of data that we can work with is limited to Python primitive data types – numbers, strings and byte sequences. To work with more sophisticated data types, such as lists, dictionaries or general objects, we need to move away from using the supplied functions.

Processing Arguments

We have already encountered the `PyArg_ParseTuple` function which "unpacks" a tuple into variables of a given C type performing the necessary Python to C conversion:

```
int PyArg_ParseTuple(PyObject *args, const char *format, ...)
```

where `format` defines the types of the Python arguments and the ... is a list of C variables of the same length as the number of format specifiers. This only works with positional parameters and the C function has to be defined in the `PyMethodDef` struct as `METH_VARARGS` which defines its signature as:

```
function(PyObject *self, PyObject *args)
```

If you try to pass a keyword parameter in Python to such a function you will see

```
TypeError: function() takes no keyword arguments
```

If you want to accept keyword parameters you need to use change the `PyMethodDef` to:

```
METH_VARARGS | METH_KEYWORDS
```

and the function's signature to

```
function(PyObject *self, PyObject *args, PyObject *kwargs)
```

where `kwargs` is a dictionary of keyword arguments which could be `NULL` if there aren't any.

With these changes you can call the function from Python with keyword parameters, but you now have to process the arguments with:

```
int PyArg_ParseTupleAndKeywords(PyObject *args, PyObject *kw,
                const char *format, char *keywords[], ...)
```

where `keywords` is an array of C strings with the names of the keyword parameters.

For example, if we want to allow keyword parameters in the `Pi` function described in the previous chapter you would need to change the `PyMethodDef` struct to:

```
static PyMethodDef AddMethods[] = {
    {"myPi", (PyCFunction) Pi,METH_VARARGS | METH_KEYWORDS,
                                        "Compute Pi"},
    {NULL, NULL, 0, NULL} // sentinel
};
```

The cast to PyCFunction is necessary to stop the compiler warning that the function has the wrong signature. With this change the function has to be redefined as:

```
static PyObject * Pi(PyObject *self, PyObject *args,
                                    PyObject *kwargs)
{
    int m, n;
    double pi,s;
    char *kw[10]={"M","N",NULL};
    if (!PyArg_ParseTupleAndKeywords(args, kwargs,
                                    "ii",kw, &m, &n))
        return NULL;
    pi=0;
    for(int k=m;k<n;k++){
        s=1;
        if(k%2==0)s=-1;
        pi=pi+s/(2*k-1);
    }
    return PyFloat_FromDouble(4*pi);
}
```

Now we have three arguments and we have to process them using PyArg_ParseTupleAndKeywords. The kw array of strings defines the keyword parameters as M and N. Notice that the order that the parameters are assigned to the variables is governed by kw. What happens is that first the positional parameters are processed and assigned in order to the variables listed. Then the keyword parameters are processed and assigned to the remaining variables in the order that the keys occur in kw. In this case M is assigned to m and N is assigned to n. If you swap the order of the keywords in kw to {"N","M"} then the N keyword parameter would be stored in m and the M keyword parameter would be stored in n, which would be confusing.

With this specification you can call pi in Python using:

```
pi=Pi.myPi(M=1,N=N)
```

or

```
pi=Pi.myPi(1,N=N)
```

or as the keyword parameters are optional even:

```
pi=Pi.myPi(1,N)
```

If you include a null string in kw then that parameter is positional only. For example, if you change kw to:

```
char *kw[10]={"","N",NULL};
```

then there has to be a single positional parameter.

If you try:

```
pi=Pi.myPi(1,N=N)
```

or

```
pi=Pi.myPi(1,N)
```

everything works, but if you try:

```
pi=Pi.myPi(M=1,N=N)
```

the result is an error:

```
TypeError: function takes at least 1 positional argument (0 given)
```

as there has to be at least one positional parameter.

If you would like to add the function's name to the error message simply add
:*name* to the end of the format string:

```
if (!PyArg_ParseTupleAndKeywords(args, kwargs, "ii:myPi",
                                               kw, &m, &n))
```

Now the error message reads;

```
TypeError: myPi() takes at least 1 positional argument (0 given)
```

You can also handle optional and keyword-only parameters using the format
string.

Adding | to the string indicates that the following items are optional. In this
case the variables should be initialized and if the parameter is missing they
will not be altered.

Adding $ to the string indicates that the following items are keyword-only
parameters which also have to be optional.

For example, changing the format from "ii" to "i|i" makes N optional either
as a keyword or positional parameter:

```
    char *kw[10]={"","N",NULL};
    n=1000;
    if (!PyArg_ParseTupleAndKeywords(args, kwargs, "i|i:myPi"
                                             ,kw, &m, &n))
        return NULL;
```

Data Formats Numbers

Of course, being able to convert a Python data type to a C data type depends
on the format specifiers that are available. There are far too many to present
each one in depth and the C SDK documentation lists them all, but there are
some general points worth making clear.

There are formats for all of the standard number types you might expect. As
Python's integer format isn't limited in size, you can convert values to
different C integer types as long as the value will fit into the C type.

The integer type specifiers are:

Checked	Unchecked	C type
b	B	unsigned char
h	H	short int
i	I	int
l		long int
	k	unsigned long
L		long long
	K	unsigned long long
	n	Py_ssize_t

These all convert a standard Python integer into the corresponding C type, with or without checking for overflow. If the value is too large to fit into the C type then the checked version returns an error:

OverflowError: Python int too large to convert to C long

You can test for an error and process the exception – see later.

There are three special cases that can be treated as integers. If you have a single character string, you can convert it to an int using "C". You can convert a single byte bytes or bytearray object to a C char using "c". Finally, the "p" format will convert a Python Boolean to a C int with 1 for True and 0 for False.

Floating point numbers don't have the same problem as integers because the Python and C types are compatible in the sense that they can both represent the same range. All you have to do is use f for float and d for double.

When it comes to complex numbers, there is a complex Python to C facility but the C complex data structure is provided by the C API. The D format specifier converts a Python complex number and stores it in a C Py_complex struct:

```
typedef struct {
    double real;
    double imag;
} Py_complex;
```

There are various complex functions of the form Py_c_operation. For example:

Py_complex_Py_c_sum(Py_complex a, Py_complex b)

returns the sum of the two complex numbers. You can convert the C complex struct into a Python complex object using:

PyObject *PyComplex_FromCComplex(Py_complex v)

You can use this to return a Python complex object.

Data Formats Strings and Bytes

The problem with strings and bytes is the need to allocate or reuse an area of memory to store the C version of the data and there is the big problem of Unicode. Raw C doesn't really support Unicode without help from a third-party library. Indeed, you can view the Unicode facilities that the Python C API provides as a Unicode library for C.

There are three ways that the different formats provide a buffer with the data for you to use:

1. Immutable objects such as strings and bytes provide a `const char*` pointer to the raw data that they contain. In this case you cannot change the data and you leave the management of the buffer to the object. Some formats treat the buffer as a null-terminated string, others also return the length of the string and so allow null bytes.

2. More sophisticated objects that support the buffer protocol, strings and bytearrays for example, can also fill a `Pybuffer` struct provided by the calling function. The `Pybuffer` has fields that allow you to work with the data. It is the responsibility of the calling program to release the `PyBuffer` by calling `PyBuffer_Release`.

3. Some formats can encode the data using a Python encoding and in this case a raw char buffer is created on the heap and it is the calling program's responsibility to call `PyMem_Free` to free the allocated buffer when it is finished using it.

You can think of this as three tiers of sophistication. The simplest being the provision of access to the object's internal raw data, followed by the buffer protocol and finally the conversion of encodings.

Raw data

The following format specifiers return a character array:

	Python Type	C Types
s	str	`const char *`
z	str or None	`const char *`
y	bytes-like object	`const char *`
s#	str, bytes-like object	`const char *`, `Py_ssize_t`
z#	str, bytes-like object or None	`const char *`, `Py_ssize_t`
y#	bytes-like object	`const char *`, `Py_ssize_t`

The bytes-like object is read only and the # versions of the formats allow embedded NULLs and return the length of the string. All of the C strings returned are UTF-8 encoded.

For example, if you pass a string to a function and convert it using the "s" format specifier then what you get back is a pointer to the data that the string contains:

```
static PyObject* stringRaw(PyObject *self, PyObject *args)
{
    char *name;
    if (!PyArg_ParseTuple(args, "s", &name))
        return NULL;
    printf("%s\n",name);
    for(int i=0;name[i];i++){
        printf("%02X ",(unsigned char)name[i]);
    }
    Py_RETURN_NONE;
}
```

This prints the string and the hex code for each of its characters. The string is null-terminated and this means that you can treat it as a C string. Notice that you are protected against the string including a NULL before its end. If this is the case a:

```
ValueError: embedded null character
```

exception is thrown. You can try out the function using:

```
import example
example.stringRaw("Hello World")
```

In this case you will see the ASCII codes for "Hello World" displayed:

```
Hello World
48 65 6C 6C 6F 20 57 6F 72 6C 64
```

This is untypical and only works because the text only uses the ASCII subset of Unicode. Python strings are coded as Unicode by default and are converted to UTF-8. For example, if you use:

```
example.stringRaw("\N{GREEK CAPITAL LETTER DELTA}")
```

this creates a UTF-8 C string with a single Greek capital delta Δ, which is coded in UTF-8 as CE 94, i.e. two bytes. The program displays:

╫╙
CE 94

which indicates that the two bytes are treated as two ASCII characters by the C program the characters you actually see correspond to codes CE and 94 which depend on what character set the terminal is using. As C knows nothing about UTF-8 this isn't unreasonable.

Multi-byte UTF-8 characters can cause a C program some problems, but notice that you cannot get a NULL inserted into a string from a UTF-8 encoding. In UTF-8 the only place a NULL byte can occur is in the coding of the first ASCII character NULL, i.e. \0.

If you need to cope with NULL characters you can use the # versions of the format specifiers, which return the length of the string:

```
static PyObject *stringRawLen(PyObject *self, PyObject *args)
{
  char *name;
  Py_ssize_t len;
  if (!PyArg_ParseTuple(args, "s#", &name, &len))
    return NULL;
  printf("%s\n", name);
  printf("%d\n", (int)len);
  for (int i = 0; i < len; i++)
  {
    printf("%02X ", (unsigned char)name[i]);
  }
  Py_RETURN_NONE;
}
```

If you pass a bytes object to the function then the coding is whatever you used to create the object. You need to think of passing a bytes object as exactly that - passing as sequence of bytes. In this case the possibility of there being an embedded NULL is much more likely and this can be a problem as a C String is not the same thing as a general bytes buffer. For example:

```
import example
example.stringRawLen("Hello \0 World")
```

displays:

```
Hello
13
48 65 6C 6C 6F 20 00 20 57 6F 72 6C 64
```

Py_Buffer

The format specifiers that return a Py_Buffer are:

	Python Type
s*	str or bytes-like object
z*	str, bytes-like object or None
y*	bytes-like object
w*	read-write bytes-like object

Although the Python type is listed as a string or bytes object, all that really matters is that the object supports the buffer protocol. Python strings are converted to UTF-8 C strings.

Returning a Py_buffer struct is very similar to simply providing a pointer to the internal buffer that the object uses. A Py_buffer struct wraps the internal buffer by providing additional information on how the buffer is organized. This additional information goes far enough to even allow the client program to modify the internal buffer.

That is, the buffer protocol provides enough information to use the internal buffer without invalidating it. The buffer structure can be very complicated with different parts of it stored in different locations, possibly with 2D structures for image storage, but most of the time the only important field is len which tells you how long the buffer is. This allows the buffer to store arbitrary byte values even if it originated as a null-terminated string. The actual data is pointed at by the buf field.

For example you can convert the previous function to work with a Py_Buffer:

```
static PyObject* stringPBuffer(PyObject *self, PyObject *args)
{
    Py_buffer myBuf;
    if (!PyArg_ParseTuple(args, "s*", &myBuf))
        return NULL;

    char *myString=(char*) myBuf.buf;
    printf("%s\n",myString);
    for(int i=0;i< myBuf.len;i++){
        printf("%02X ",(unsigned char)myString[i]);
    }
    PyBuffer_Release(&myBuf);
    Py_RETURN_NONE;
}
```

Notice that we convert the pointer to the internal buffer myBuf.buf which is a pointer to void to a pointer to char so that we can treat it as a C string. However, the for loop makes use of the buffer's length rather than a null termination. There is no exception if the string includes a NULL. For example:

```
example.stringPBuffer("Hello \0 World")
```

displays:

```
Hello
48 65 6C 6C 6F 20 00 20 57 6F 72 6C 64
```

The encoding of the internal buffer depends on the object that supports the buffer protocol. In the case of a string the encoding is UTF-8 and for a bytes or byte array object it is just a series of bytes.

We also have to use PyBuffer_Release to let the Python object know we have finished using the buffer. The client program "owns" the Py_buffer struct, but the Python object continues to own and look after the internal buffer.

Encoders

The encoder format specifiers are:

	Python Type	CType
es	str	const char *encoding, char **buffer
et	str, bytes or bytearray	const char *encoding, char **buffer
es#	str	const char *encoding, char **buffer, Py_ssize_t *buffer_length
et#	str, bytes or bytearray	const char *encoding, char **buffer, Py_ssize_t *buffer_length

The # versions allow for embedded NULLs and return the length of the buffer and the et versions don't perform any encoding, they simply assume that the data is already in the specified coding and return the raw data.

The encoding converters are in some senses the most complex of the conversion formats, but they also return the simplest data structure – a raw C buffer. To understand how they work you need to know about encodings in general and this is covered in detail in Chapter 10.

All Python strings can represent any of the huge range of Unicode characters. The problem is that not everything uses pure Unicode and there are a number of different ways of encoding the same information. For example, UTF-8 uses a variable number of bytes to represent the full range of Unicode. Before Unicode there was a system of "code pages" which reused the single byte range of extended ASCII to encode multiple characters. Python supports all of the old Window code pages and their ANSI standardizations.

To convert a Unicode sequence into a particular encoding you can use one of the "e" format specifiers. For example, es converts a string to an encoded C string using the encoding specified by the first variable in the parameter list. That is:

```
"es", "cp1252", &name
```

encodes the string according to cp1252 which is Code Page 1252, i.e. the Latin code page for Windows and stores a pointer to the result in name. The result is stored in a *char buffer which is allocated by the API. You have to tell the Python API to free the buffer when you are finished using it by calling PyMem_Free().

A function to encode a string or byte sequence into the Latin code page is:

```
static PyObject *stringEncode(PyObject *self, PyObject *args)
{
  char *name = NULL;
  if (!PyArg_ParseTuple(args, "es", "cp1252", &name))
    return NULL;
  printf("%s \n",  name);
  for (int i = 0;  name[i]; i++)
  {
    printf("%02X ", (unsigned char)name[i]);
  }
  PyMem_Free(name);
  Py_RETURN_NONE;
}
```

If you try this out using:

```
example.stringEncode("Hello World")
```

then you will see "Hello World" followed by the usual ASCII codes for each character. This isn't a good test as the encoding doesn't change any of the ASCII characters into anything else. To see that the encoding is actually changing something, try:

```
example.stringEncode("\u2020")
```

Unicode character 0x2020 is †, i.e. a dagger symbol, and this doesn't occur in the ASCII code, but it is character 0x86 in the Latin code page. If you run the program above you will probably see:

åå

86

The 86 corresponds to the code for the dagger in the Latin code page – the character you see printed depends on what code page the editor's terminal is using. In the example above it is the Windows terminal which uses code page 850 Latin-1 by default and code 0x86 is "Lower case a with ring above". You can see that the Unicode dagger has been converted to the correct code page code, but what you actually see depends on what code page or Unicode the terminal is set to.

This is confusing and it is the reason Unicode and encodings such as UTF-8 have become standard.

If a Unicode symbol doesn't have a representation within the selected code page then an exception occurs. If you want to substitute a "character not found" symbol you need to handle the exception.

To make use of other Python encoders you may have to swap to a format that allows NULLs. For example, to encode a string to UTF-16, a variable length encoding using 16-bit words, you have to use the function with es#:

```
static PyObject *stringEncode2(PyObject *self, PyObject *args)
{
  char *name = NULL;
  Py_ssize_t len;
  if (!PyArg_ParseTuple(args, "es#", "utf-16", &name, &len))
    return NULL;
  printf("%s \n",  name);
  for (int i = 0;  i<len; i++)
  {
    printf("%02X ", (unsigned char)name[i]);
  }
  PyMem_Free(name);
  Py_RETURN_NONE;
}
```

In this case you also have to supply a variable to record the length of the string.

When using es# you have the option of preallocating the buffer before calling the PyArg_ParseTuple function. In this case the buffer will be filled with the data and you are responsible for freeing it. For example:

```
static PyObject *stringEncodeAllocate(PyObject *self,
                                      PyObject *args)
{
  Py_ssize_t len = 25;
  char *name = malloc(sizeof(char) * (len + 1));

  if (!PyArg_ParseTuple(args, "es#", "cp1252", &name, &len))
    return NULL;
  printf("%d\n", (int)len);
  printf("%s \n", name);
  for (int i = 0; i < len; i++)
  {
    printf("%02X ", (unsigned char)name[i]);
  }
  free(name);
  Py_RETURN_NONE;
}
```

Notice that we now use free rather than PyMem_Free as Python doesn't own the buffer. The len parameter gives the number of characters in the string and it is null-terminated even if it has embedded NULLs. If the buffer isn't big enough an exception is raised.

For more details on how to work with Unicode strings see Chapter 10.

Sequences

Dealing with more complex Python objects requires more than format specifiers. However, if an object is a sequence then you can extract the data it contains. A sequence is a "container" for a range of other, usually simpler, data types so that they can be accessed by an integer index. If you want to know more about this see *Programmer's Python: Everything is Data*, ISBN: 9781871962757. You cannot use a format to convert a sequence into something equivalent in C such as a struct or an array, but you can convert each of the elements in the sequence – providing they are simple.

If you enclose format specifiers in parentheses then it is assumed that the items are derived from a sequence. For example:

```
(dis)
```

means that the first element is a double, next an integer and next a string. This would unpack a tuple or a list or any sequence into three C variables of the correct type. You can also nest parentheses to handle elements which are themselves sequences. For example:

(d(ii))

means that the first element is a double and the second is a sequence with a pair of integers e.g. $(3.14,(1,2))$.

For example, if we have a sequence that has an integer first element followed by a pair of doubles and then a string we can unpack this into C variables using:

```
static PyObject *sequenceElements(PyObject *self, PyObject *args)
{
  int number;
  double x,y;
  char *name = NULL;

  if (!PyArg_ParseTuple(args, "(idds)", &number,&x,&y, &name))
    return NULL;
  printf("%d %f %f %s",number,x,y,name);

  Py_RETURN_NONE;
}
```

If you call this using:

```
import example
example.sequenceElements((2,1.2,1.3,"test"))
```

then you will see displayed:

```
2 1.200000 1.300000 test
```

If you replace the tuple with a list then it still works.

If the two doubles are formed into a tuple then we can still extract them by changing the format to:

```
if (!PyArg_ParseTuple(args, "(i(dd)s)", &number,&x,&y, &name))
```

With this change you can call the function using:

```
import example
example.sequenceElements((2,(1.2,1.3),"test"))
```

The types of the C variables have to match the format specifier and this means that if the sequence you pass in doesn't match the format you will generate a TypeError exception.

While this is a way of getting lists and tuples into your C function, notice that it only works for "short" sequences because you have to create a C variable for each item. If you want to convert a list or tuple with an arbitrary number of elements you are going to have to do the job yourself.

A complete listing of all of the functions given in this chapter, together with test Python code, can be found on the book's webpage at www.iopress.info.

Summary

- A very standard task is to convert Python objects passed in to an extension function to C data types.

- The workhorse function for this is `PyArg_ParseTuple` which can convert a range of basic data types from Python to C.

- As well as positional arguments, it is easy to support keyword arguments by changing the argument type in `PyMethodDef` to include `METH_KEYWORDS`

- To process positional and keyword arguments use `PyArg_ParseTupleAndKeywords` which works in the same way as `PyArg_ParseTuple`.

- The simplest conversions are from Python numbers to C numbers – integer, float and complex.

- Converting Python strings to C strings is more complicated because Python supports Unicode and C does not without the help of additional libraries.

- You can use encoders to translate from Unicode to older encodings and standard encodings such as UTF-8.

- The same techniques can be used to convert containers such as lists and tuples can also be converted into C data types as long as the elements are basic data types.

Chapter 6
Returning Python Objects

A C API function has a fixed signature and has to return a pointer to a
`PyObject`. Even if your function is going to return nothing at all it still has to
return a pointer to a `PyObject`. This generally means that you have to
convert a C data type into a `PyObject` and this is easier than you might
imagine. It is also the first step on the road to creating your own completely
new Python objects.

Py_BuildValue

The `Py_BuldValue` function is best regarded as the inverse of the
`PyArg_ParseTuple` function:

```
*Py_Object = Py_BuildValue(format,variables)
```

It takes a format string and a list of C variables and converts the C data types
into Python data types as instructed by the format string. The format
specifiers are very similar, but not identical, to the ones used with
`PyArg_ParseTuple`. It is also similar in the sense that it can return a tuple of
Python data types, but it can also return a single `PyObject`. If you specify a
single format and variable then it returns a single Python object.

If you specify multiple formats and variables then it returns a tuple of
Python objects. If you put a format string in parentheses then a tuple is
always returned. The number of variables has to match the number of
format items.

If you pass an empty string as the format then the Python object `None` is
returned by the function. You can use this as the return value in an
extension function which doesn't return a value:

```
return Py_BuildValue("");
```

In practice it is probably better to use the macro which includes the return:

```
Py_RETURN_NONE;
```

Notice that the extension function is responsible for cleaning up any
memory that it allocates after using it in `Py_BuildValue` to construct a
Python object. The Python object constructed does not make use of any of
the data storage in the variables used to construct it. That is, the Python
object is created for you on the heap and any data it is to contain is copied

from the C variable. This means that if the variables are automatic, i.e. allocated on the stack, you don't have to do anything, but if they are allocated on the heap you need to free them before returning.

The same issue occurs with respect to the Python object you are working with. In this case we have to tell the Python system how long they should live by manipulating their reference counts, see Chapter 7.

Numbers

Numbers are the simplest thing to return from a function. This is especially true as Python integers can't overflow, so all C Integer types can be converted to Python integers without fear of overflow.

The standard integer formats are:

	C Type
i	int
b	char
h	short int
l	long int
L	long long
n	Py_ssize_t

All of these are for signed values. To convert unsigned values you simply use the uppercase letter or k for unsigned long and K for unsigned long long. Notice that the value of the Python integer depends on the C type and the type that you indicate that it is. For example:

```
static PyObject *retInt(PyObject *self, PyObject *args)
{
  int value=-1;
  return Py_BuildValue("I",value);
}
```

If you try this out:

```
import example
print(example.retInt())
```

you will see, not -1, but 4294967295. The reason for this is that this is the way -1 is represented in two's-complement form and the I format specifier forces it to be interpreted as an unsigned number hence not -1 but a positive number.

If the C data was stored on the heap then it is the responsibility of the extension function to free it. For example:

```
static PyObject *retInt(PyObject *self, PyObject *args)
{
  int *value = malloc(sizeof(int));
  *value = 42;
  PyObject *temp = Py_BuildValue("i", *value);
  free(value);
  return temp;
}
```

Notice that now we have to store the pointer to the constructed PyObject, free the allocated memory and then return the pointer.

You can also convert a C int or char into a bytes object or a string of length-1. The format c converts a char and C converts an int.

The same is true of Python's floating point type in that it is double precision and so C's double or float can be converted to it without loss of precision or overflow:

d	double
f	float

You can also convert a C complex struct to a Python complex object using the D format. Note that the C complex struct is already provided by Python, i.e. it is a Py_complex struct.

C Strings

You can convert a C string to a Unicode Python string using the format codes: s, U or z.

For example:

```
static PyObject *strTostr(PyObject *self, PyObject *args)
{
  char *name="Brian";
  return Py_BuildValue("s",name);
}
```

when used from Python:

```
print(example.strTostr())
```

displays Brian.

The documentation says that this converts the UTF-8 C string into a Unicode Python string. If the C string is encoded in any other way the result is likely not to work, but UTF-8 is not a native format for C. If you want to use it you either have to use a third-party library or manually encode it yourself.

For example:

```c
static PyObject *strTostr2(PyObject *self, PyObject *args)
{
  char name[]="    Brian";
  name[0]=0xCE;
  name[1]=0x94;
  return Py_BuildValue("s",name);
}
```

inserts a 2-byte UTF-8 code for a Greek capital delta Δ to the start of the string. This displays:

Δ Brian

As long as you work in UTF-8 in C, then the Python string will be Unicode.

If you need to include NULLs in the string, or just want to return part of the string, you can use s#, U# or z# and supply the length of the string:

```c
static PyObject *strTostrLen(PyObject *self, PyObject *args)
{
  char name[] = "    Brian";
  Py_ssize_t len = 5;
  name[0] = 0xCE;
  name[1] = 0x94;
  return Py_BuildValue("s#", name, len);
}
```

This displays:

Δ Br

which is clearly only four characters not five as len would suggest. The reason is that the C length specification is in terms of bytes not characters. The first character, the Greek capital delta is coded as two bytes in UTF-8 and has length two.

The y and y# format specifiers can be used to convert a C string to a bytes object with the # form specifying the length. The bytes object is simply a copy of the bytes in the string with no encoding, for example:

```c
static PyObject *strTobytesLen(PyObject *self, PyObject *args)
{
  char name[] = "    Brian";
  Py_ssize_t len = 5;
  name[0] = 0xCE;
  name[1] = 0x94;
  return Py_BuildValue("y#", name, len);
}
```

If you run:

```python
print(example.strTobytesLen())
```

you will see:

b'\xce\x94 Br'

that is, the exact sequence of bytes that were in the string.

Wide Character Strings

As Python works using Unicode it makes sense for the C extension function to work in an encoding such as UTF-8, but C has no built-in features to make this possible. C does provide a wchar_t, i.e. wide character, type which is either a two or four bytes and is used to store UTF-16- or UTF-32-encoded characters. However, apart from providing the type there is very little in standard C that helps you use either UTF-16 or UTF-32.

If you want to work with wchar_t then there are two formats that will convert the UTF-16 or UTF-32 to a Python Unicode string u and u# with the u# also setting the length of the string, for example:

```
static PyObject *wcharTostrLen(PyObject *self, PyObject *args)
{
    wchar_t name[] = L"    Brian";
    Py_ssize_t len = 5;
    name[0] = 0x0394;
    return Py_BuildValue("u#", name, len);
}
```

Notice that now we have to encode the Greek capital delta using UTF-16, which is different from the two byte UTF-8. If you try this out you will find that you do get exactly five characters in the Python string:

Δ Br

In this case each 2-byte character counts as one Unicode character. However, this is not generally true. The problem is that UTF-16 is a variable byte format like UTF-8 and there are characters that need two 16 bit-words to be represented. The only characters that can be represented in a single word are in the Basic Multilingual Plane, BMP. While this is often sufficient, it rules out many emojis.

For example, if you want to use the Zipper-Mouth Face character then you have to use two 16-bit values;

```
static PyObject *wcharTostrLen2(PyObject *self, PyObject *args)
{
  wchar_t name[] =L"    Brian";
  Py_ssize_t len = 5;
  name[0] =0xD83E;
  name[1]=0xDD10;
  return Py_BuildValue("u#", name, len);
}
```

and this displays:

😐 Br

and again we only have four characters because the first uses two elements of the wchar_t array. Notice the use of L in front of the string to ensure that the *char literal is converted to wchar_t.

Note: At the time of writing *wcharTostrLen2* doesn't work on Linux with a full 16-bit word.

Tuples, Lists and Dictionaries

There are also format specifiers which allow you to return multiple simple data values packaged as tuples, lists or dictionaries. If you surround a format with parentheses () then a tuple is constructed. If you surround a format with square brackets [] then a list is constructed and if you surround a format with curly brackets {} a dictionary is constructed. If you create a dictionary then the C types are taken in pairs, the first one the key and the second the value.

So to construct a tuple:

```
static PyObject *retTuple(PyObject *self, PyObject *args)
{
  int number = 42;
  double x = 1.2, y = 1.1;
  char *name = "brian";

  return Py_BuildValue("(isdd)", number, name, x, y);
}
```

This returns:

```
(42, 'brian', 1.2, 1.1)
```

In this case the parentheses are not needed as a multi-element format defaults to a tuple.

To create a list we just change the parentheses to square brackets:

```
static PyObject *retList(PyObject *self, PyObject *args)
{
  int number = 42;
  double x = 1.2, y = 1.1;
  char *name = "brian";

  return Py_BuildValue("[isdd]", number, name, x, y);
}
```

This returns:

```
[42, 'brian', 1.2, 1.1]
```

and in this case the brackets are required.

To create a dictionary:

```
static PyObject *retDict(PyObject *self, PyObject *args)
{
  int number = 42;
  double x = 1.2, y = 1.1;
  char *name = "brian";

  return Py_BuildValue("{sisssdsd}", "first", number,
                          "second", name,"x", x,"y", y);
}
```

This returns:

```
{'first': 42, 'second': 'brian', 'x': 1.2, 'y': 1.1}
```

Notice that the format specifier has to include a term for each of the keys as well as for the values.

As in the case of processing arguments, this is a way of constructing sequences with only a few elements. To create lists or arrays with lots of elements we have to do the job manually.

A complete listing of all of the functions given in this chapter, together with test Python code, can be found on the book's webpage at www.iopress.info.

Summary

- The `Py_BuildValue` function is best regarded as the inverse of the `PyArg_ParseTuple` function. It takes C data and, using a format specifier, converts them to Python objects.

- If there is more than one C variable, it creates a tuple of objects.

- An extension function always has to return a `*PyObject`. If it has no return value it should return `None` by using `Py_RETURN_NONE`

- Numeric values are easy to convert because Python's integer type can store any C value and floats are compatible.

- Strings are more of a problem because C uses ASCII and Python uses Unicode. Generally you have to convert between UTF-8 and Unicode.

- C does support wide character `wchar_t` types to support Unicode or UTF-16, at least in theory. There are format specifiers that convert UTF-16 to Unicode.

- More complex data types need special treatment, but tuples, lists and dictionaries can be created from simpler C types.

Chapter 7
Objects And Attributes

So far we have been working with primitive data – numbers, strings, bytes and so on. These can easily be converted to C data types, worked with and then converted back to Python types for the extension function to return. However, not all Python objects are primitive data and we need to extend what we do to include them. In this chapter we look at how to work with a general Python object that is passed to the extension function.

Object Arguments

The first thing we have to deal with is how to get a general Python object into the extension function. The extension function is always passed a tuple of arguments and we could use Python functions to unpack the tuple manually to get `PyObject` pointers but the `PyArg_ParseTuple` function is still easier to use.

There are three format specifiers that work with general objects:

- ◆ O stores a `PyObject` in the specified variable. The object belongs to Python and is managed by Python.

- ◆ O! works like O but you can specify the type of object. A `TypeError` is raised if the argument isn't of this type.

- ◆ O& calls a converter function to perform a conversion of the Python object to a C data type.

Of the three we will use O to return a `PyObject` pointer without checking or conversion. For example:

```
PyObject *myObject;
if (!PyArg_ParseTuple(args, "O", &myObject)
    return NULL;
```

stores a pointer to the general Python object in `myObject` and this works irrespective of the type of the object and no conversion is performed.

Reference Counting

Now that we are creating new Python objects in C and working with attributes we need to consider their lifetime. If the C function creates a Python object then it is created by the Python system and it allocates the memory on the heap. That is, when a C function creates a Python object it is just as if that object had been created as part of the Python program.

Python uses a system of reference counting to decide when a Python object can be removed. Each time a Python variable is set to reference an object the object's reference count is incremented and whenever a variable that references an object no longer references the object the reference count is decremented.

Thus the reference count reflects the number of variables that reference the object and when this is zero the object is inaccessible and can be removed from memory, i.e. it can be garbage-collected.

Using reference counting for garbage collection is efficient, but it only works if the reference counts are updated correctly. If the reference count is zero and there is still a variable referencing the object it will be garbage-collected and when the variable is used there will be an error. If the reference count is non-zero and there are no variables referencing the object then we have a memory leak.

This is the simplest case, but things can be more complex and Chapter 13 deals with the problem of cyclic references where objects can be inaccessible while still having non-zero reference counts. For the moment we concentrate on keeping reference counts accurate as this is a requirement for any garbage collection.

When programming in Python the reference count is automatically updated as variables change what they reference. If `myvar` references `myObject` then `myvar = myObject2` decrements `myObject1`'s reference count and increments `myObject2`'s.

Creating and accessing Python objects in C creates a problem as C references are not part of the Python reference counting system. Most of the time this is not a problem as the C function is isolated and doesn't need to take part in the reference counting.

For example, when a Python object is passed into a function the fact that the function now has a reference to the Python object is usually irrelevant as when the function returns the C reference is lost and reference count that Python had for the object is correct when the function returns.

That is, if there were three variables referencing `myObject` before the function call, there are three variables referencing `myObject` after the function call.

This use of a Python object without incrementing the reference count is called borrowing a reference. It works because the reference that the C function creates is destroyed when it comes to an end. If this isn't the case then you probably do need to increment the reference count.

If you create a Python object while in a C function then the Python system creates the object for you and sets its reference count to one. In most cases functions that return references to existing Python objects automatically increment the reference count. There are exceptions, however. Notably `PyTuple_GetItem()`, `PyList_GetItem()`, `PyDict_GetItem()` do not increment, but confusingly their general object equivalent `PyObject_GetItem` does increase the reference count. Working with Python objects with collections such as lists, tuple and dictionaries is perhaps the most confusing of all because the `get` and `set` functions try to make things easier for you by either incrementing or not incrementing the reference count.

You can check to see what a function does in the documentation. A function that does increment is labeled:

`Return value: New Reference`

whereas a function that does not is labeled:

`Return value: Borrowed Reference.`

If you return an object as part of the result of a function then its reference count should be one more than when the function started with the Python variable you are assigning it to being the extra reference.

If you are not returning the object to Python then you have to decrement the reference count of any new reference unless you plan on storing a pointer to it in a static variable so that the function can use it when subsequently called. The reason is simply that in most cases the C reference is lost when the function ends and the count has to reflect this.

You can modify the reference count using:

- `void Py_INCREF(PyObject *o)`
- `void Py_XINCREF(PyObject *o)`
- `void Py_DECREF(PyObject *o)`
- `void Py_XDECREF(PyObject *o)`

The X versions of the functions increment or decrement the reference count but don't mind if the object `o` is `NULL` when nothing happens.

You can also use:

- void Py_CLEAR(PyObject *o)

to safely decrement a reference count and remove the reference. It is equivalent to:

```
PyObject *tmp = o;
if (tmp != NULL) {
        o = NULL;
        Py_DECREF(tmp);
}
```

You should always remove the reference before decrementing the reference count to avoid complicated errors due to interactions with garbage collection.

Whenever you create a Python object or get a reference to a Python object, the question is have you increased the number of references that persist when the C program ends? If the answer is yes then the reference count should be incremented. If the answer is no then it should not be incremented.

This is a simple principle, but unfortunately the C API confuses the issue by sometimes doing the increment for you and sometimes not, depending on the expected common use case for the function. So in practice you have to know if the function you used to create or get the object has automatically incremented the reference count for you.

You can check what an objects reference count is in Python using

```
print(sys.getrefcount(object))
```

Notice that the returned value is one more than the current reference count because getrefcount adds a reference to object while it is running. You can check the reference count in C using:

```
Py_REFCNT(object)
```

It reports the accurate current reference count. See the section at the end of Chapter 9 for more details of making use of these. In practice you do need to check that reference counts are what you expect them to be when your C function terminates.

Attributes

Now we have a pointer to a `PyObject` what can we do with it? In nearly all cases what you do to objects is access, and perhaps modify, their attributes. In Python an attribute of an object is a dictionary key/value that can be accessed using "dot" notation, that is:

```
object.attribute
```

is the same as:

```
object["attribute"]
```

and you can get or set its value, which can be any other Python object, but is often a simple primitive data type.

So how do we get an object's attribute in C?

The answer is we use

```
PyObject *PyObject_GetAttr(PyObject *o, PyObject *attr_name)
```

this returns a `PyObject` pointer to the attribute specified by `attr_name` and increments its reference count. Notice that `attr_name` is specified as a `PyObject`. This isn't unreasonable as this is a Python function and so we should expect it to require a Python string to specify the name of the attribute. This means we need to construct a Python string to make use of it.

We already know one way to do this using `Py_BuildValue`:

```
PyObject *attribName = Py_BuildValue("s", "myAttribute1");
```

There are functions to convert C types to Python types and these are introduced later.

We can now get the value of the attribute:

```
PyObject *myAtt1 = PyObject_GetAttr(myObject, attribName);
```

Notice that the value of the attribute is again a Python object. This can be used in other Python functions, but if you want to use it in a C program without the help of Python functions you need to convert and how to do this depends on its type.

Putting all this together gives:

```
static PyObject *Attributes1(PyObject *self, PyObject *args)
{
  PyObject *myObject;
  if (!PyArg_ParseTuple(args, "O", &myObject))
    return NULL;
  PyObject *attribName = Py_BuildValue("s", "myAttribute1");
  PyObject *myAtt1 = PyObject_GetAttr(myObject, attribName);

  Py_XDECREF(attribName);
  return myAtt1;
}
```

Notice that we have to decrement the reference count of `attribName` to make sure that it is garbage-collected after the C function has finished. However, we don't need to decrement the reference count of `myAtt1` as this is the returned value which needs a reference count of one.

If you try this out:

```
import example

class myClass:
    myAttribute1=10
    myAttribute2="Brian"

myInstance=myClass()
print(example.Attributes1(myInstance))
```

you should see 10 displayed as you would expect.

The task of converting a C string to a Python string simply to access an attribute is so common that there is a shortcut:

```
PyObject *PyObject_GetAttrString(PyObject *o,
                                      const char *attr_name)
```

this accepts a C string as the attribute's name and performs the conversion for you. For example, using this the above function can be written:

```
static PyObject *Attributes1(PyObject *self, PyObject *args)
{
  PyObject *myObject;
  if (!PyArg_ParseTuple(args, "O", &myObject))
    return NULL;

  PyObject *myAtt1 = PyObject_GetAttrString(myObject,
                                        "myAttribute1");
  return myAtt1;
}
```

Notice that as we are returning `myAtt1` we do not need to decrement its reference count as it needs to persist in the Python program.

If we want to work with attributes in C we need to convert the Python objects into C data types and there are functions provided for just this purpose.

Numbers

As always, numbers are the basic primitives and there are several functions which convert a C `long`, which is usually the same size as `int`, or `long long` into a Python `int`. As a Python `int` doesn't have a limit there is no chance of overflow. All of the C to Python function have `From` in their names and they all set the reference count of the Python object to one:

- `PyLong_FromLong(long v)`
- `PyLong_FromUnsignedLong(unsigned long v)`
- `PyLong_FromLongLong(long long v)`
- `PyLong_FromUnsignedLongLong(unsigned long long v)`
- `PyLong_FromSsize_t(Py_ssize_t v)`
- `PyLong_FromSize_t(size_t v)`

As well as these integer-to-integer conversions, there are two other functions to add to the list:

- `PyLong_FromDouble(double v)`
- `PyLong_FromString(const char *str, char **pend, int base)`

The former returns a Python int constructed from the integer part of the C `double` and the latter parses the C string and constructs a Python int. The string has to hold a valid integer and `pend` is set to the character following the number. If `pend` is non-null when the function is called this is taken as the start of the number in the string. You can specify the base that the number is in or set it to zero for default behavior. Leading spaces between a base specifier and digits are ignored. If the string cannot be converted it raises a `ValueError`.

There is also:

- `PyObject *PyLong_FromUnicodeObject(PyObject *u, int base)`

which converts a Python string into a Python integer.

The functions that convert a Python `integer` to C `int` all have `As` in their name:

- `long PyLong_AsLong(PyObject *obj)`
- `long PyLong_AsLongAndOverflow(PyObject *obj, int *overflow)`
- `unsigned long PyLong_AsUnsignedLong(PyObject *pylong)`
- `unsigned long PyLong_AsUnsignedLongMask(PyObject *obj)`

and there is a similar set of functions which convert to a C `long long`:

- `long long PyLong_AsLongLong(PyObject *obj)`
- `long long PyLong_AsLongLongAndOverflow(PyObject *obj,`
  `                                        int *overflow)`
- `unsigned long long PyLong_AsUnsignedLongLong(`
  `                                        PyObject *pylong)`
- `unsigned long long PyLong_AsUnsignedLongLongMask(`
  `                                        PyObject *obj)`

Functions with `Overflow` in their names set the overflow parameter to `1` or `-1` in response to a positive or negative overflow. The functions with `Mask` in their names simply wrap the value if it is too big to fit into the variable.

The only complication is that if there is an error these functions return `-1`, which is indistinguishable from a valid result and so you need to use `PyErr_Occurred()` to detect an error see Chapter 9.

Two functions return a `C` types from a Python `int`:

- `Py_ssize_t PyLong_AsSsize_t(PyObject *pylong)`
- `double PyLong_AsDouble(PyObject *pylong)`

Finally there are two very specialized functions which allow you to get a Python representation of a pointer and vice versa:

- `void *PyLong_AsVoidPtr(PyObject *pylong)`
- `PyObject *PyLong_FromVoidPtr(void *p)`

Converting between `floats` follows a similar pattern. Functions with `From` in their names convert from C types and those with `As` in their names convert to Python types.

- `PyObject *PyFloat_FromDouble(double v)`
- `double PyFloat_AsDouble(PyObject *pyfloat)`

There is also:

- `double PyFloat_AS_DOUBLE(PyObject *pyfloat)`

which does no error checking. If anything goes wrong the "As" functions return `NULL`.

As with integers, you can convert a Python string to a Python float and then presumably to a C `double` if that's what you need:

- `PyObject *PyFloat_FromString(PyObject *str)`

There are functions to convert complex values:

- `PyObject *PyComplex_FromCComplex(Py_complex v)`
- `Py_complex PyComplex_AsCComplex(PyObject *op)`

Recall that `Py_complex` is the C struct provided by the API to represent complex values and `PyComplex` is the Python complex object. To create a Python complex value from the real and imaginary parts as C doubles:

- `PyObject *PyComplex_FromDoubles(double real, double imag)`

and you can get the real and imaginary parts as C doubles:

- `double PyComplex_RealAsDouble(PyObject *op)`
- `double PyComplex_ImagAsDouble(PyObject *op)`

If the object isn't a Python complex object then __complex__ is called to get a complex value representation.

If the Python object used in any of the conversion functions isn't of the correct type then a conversion to the correct type is attempted. If a complex value is needed then __complex__ is called to get a complex representation, followed by __float__ to get a floating point representation and finally an __index__ to get an integer value. Similarly if a float is required __float__ and __index__ are called and if an int is required __index__ is called.

There is also a function to convert a long to a Python Boolean:

- ◆ PyBool_FromLong(long v)

and it returns a pointer to one of:

```
Py_False
Py_True
```

These are subclasses of Python integers with just two values, but you shouldn't make use of how they are defined. Instead you should use:

- ◆ Py_IsTrue(PyObject *bool)
- ◆ Py_IsFalse(PyObject *bool)

to test their value. You can also use:

- ◆ Py_RETURN_FALSE
- ◆ Py_RETURN_TRUE

to return a Python True or False from a C function.

There are also functions to test to see if a PyObject is a particular type of number object:

- ◆ PyBool_Check(PyObject *o)
- ◆ PyLong_Check(PyObject *p)
- ◆ PyFloat_Check(PyObject *p)
- ◆ PyComplex_Check(PyObject *p)

Each returns True if the object is of the specified type or a sub-type. If you want to test for the type and not the sub-type then you can use:

- ◆ PyLong_CheckExact(PyObject *p)
- ◆ PyFloat_CheckExact(PyObject *p)
- ◆ PyComplex_CheckExact(PyObject *p)
- ◆ PyBool_Check(PyObject *o)

String Attributes

The whole subject of working with strings is a big one and covered in detail in Chapter 10, but the most common operation is to take a Unicode Python string and convert it into a C UTF-8 formatted string and vice versa. The reason that UTF-8 is important is that, as long as the Python program restricts itself to ASCII, the resulting C string is a perfectly standard ASCII-coded C string. Similarly a standard ASCII C string can be represented as a Python Unicode string by treating it as if it was UTF-8 encoded.

To convert a C string into a Python Unicode string:

```
PyObject *PyUnicode_FromString(const char *u)
```

or

```
PyObject *PyUnicode_DecodeUTF8(const char *s, Py_ssize_t size,
                                         const char *errors)
```

This takes a UTF-8 C string and converts it into a Python string with reference count of one. The errors parameter determines what should happen if encoding isn't possible. Passing NULL sets the default behavior of raising a ValueError if a character cannot be represented.

To convert from a Python Unicode string to a C null-terminated UTF-8 string you can use either:

```
const char *PyUnicode_AsUTF8AndSize(PyObject *unicode,
                                         Py_ssize_t *size)
```

or

```
const char *PyUnicode_AsUTF8(PyObject *unicode)
```

The only difference is that the first returns the length of the string, which is useful if there are embedded NULLs. The string returned is always terminated by a NULL and this is not included in the length.

You can also check that an object is a Unicode string using:

- PyUnicode_Check(PyObject *o)
- PyUnicode_CheckExact(PyObject *o)

The first returns True if the object is a Unicode string or a subtype and the second only returns True if it isn't a subtype of Unicode string.

As an example of working with attribute values including strings consider the function:

```
static PyObject *displayAttributes(PyObject *self, PyObject *args)
{
  PyObject *myObject;
  PyObject *myString;
  if (!PyArg_ParseTuple(args, "OO", &myObject, &myString))
    return NULL;
  PyObject *myAtt1 = PyObject_GetAttr(myObject, myString);
  if (PyUnicode_Check(myAtt1))
  {
    const char *mytext = PyUnicode_AsUTF8(myAtt1);
    printf("%s\n", mytext);
  }
  if (PyLong_Check(myAtt1))
  {
    int myValue = PyLong_AsLong(myAtt1);
    printf("%d\n", myValue);
  }
  return myAtt1;
}
```

In this function we pass the object and attribute to be retrieved as a string. This is a Python string so it can be used in `PyObject_GetAttr` without conversion. Then we check to see if the attribute is an integer or a string and convert and print it accordingly:

```
import example

class myClass:
    myAttribute1=10
    myAttribute2="Brian"

myInstance=myClass()
value=example.displayAttributes(myInstance,"myAttribute1")
print(value)
value=example.displayAttributes(myInstance,"myAttribute2")
print(value)
```

If you try this out, you will see 10,10, Brian, Brian displayed.

Set Attributes

Now that we know how to create primitive Python data objects from C data types we can use this to set attributes on objects.

As there are get attribute functions there are also set attribute functions:

- ◆ int PyObject_SetAttr(PyObject *o, PyObject *attr_name, PyObject *v)
- ◆ int PyObject_SetAttrString(PyObject *o, const char *attr_name, PyObject *v)

The only difference between them is how you specify the attribute name – Python string or C string. The attribute has to be set to a Python object rather than a C data type and this means we need usually need to perform a conversion. An exception is raised and -1 returned if there is an error.

A subtle point is that setting an attribute automatically decrements the reference count of the object that is being replaced. For example:

```
static PyObject *Attributes2(PyObject *self, PyObject *args)
{
  PyObject *myObject;
  if (!PyArg_ParseTuple(args, "O", &myObject))
    return NULL;
  PyObject *newValue = PyLong_FromLong(42);
  if (PyObject_SetAttrString(myObject, "myAttribute1", newValue))
    return NULL;
  Py_RETURN_NONE;
}
```

sets the attribute "myAttribute1" to the integer 42. If the set attribute function fails an exception is raised and a NULL returned. The reference count of the object that was referenced by myAttribute1 is decreased by one and the new value has a reference count of one.

To see that this works, try:

```
import example
class myClass:
 myAttribute1=10
 myAttribute2="Brian"
example.Attributes2(myInstance)
print(myInstance.myAttribute1)
```

which displays 42.

Notice that an attribute can be set to any Python object.

Working With Attributes

As well as being able to get and set attributes, there are functions that let you test and manipulate them.

You can delete an attribute using:

- ◆ `int PyObject_DelAttr(PyObject *o, PyObject *attr_name)`
- ◆ `int PyObject_DelAttrString(PyObject *o,`
       `const char *attr_name)`

The first uses a Python string to identify the attribute and the second a C string. The reference count of the object deleted is decremented.

It is often important to test if an object has an attribute before you attempt to use it. There are two functions that do this:

- ◆ `int PyObject_HasAttr(PyObject *o, PyObject *attr_name)`
- ◆ `int PyObject_HasAttrString(PyObject *o,`
       `const char *attr_name)`

The first uses a Python string to identify the attribute and the second a C string. For example:

```
static PyObject *Attributes3(PyObject *self, PyObject *args)
{
  PyObject *myObject;
  if (!PyArg_ParseTuple(args, "O", &myObject))
    return NULL;
  if( PyObject_HasAttrString(myObject,"myAttribute1")){
    PyObject *myAtt1 = PyObject_GetAttrString(myObject,
                                          "myAttribute1");
    if (PyLong_Check(myAtt1))
    {
      int myValue = PyLong_AsLong(myAtt1);
      printf("%d\n", myValue);
    }
  }
   Py_RETURN_NONE;
}
```

We check that the object passed has `myAttribute1` and then check that it is an `int` before converting it and displaying the value.

Instance Testing - Advanced

It is sometimes faster to check that an object is an instance of a class or a subclass:

```
int PyObject_IsInstance(PyObject *inst, PyObject *cls)
```

Once you know that an object is an instance of a class you can assume it has all of the attributes that the class defines, unless some have been deleted which is not common. The problem with attempting this approach in a C extension function is finding the Python class object, cls.

When your extension object runs the current module is whatever you called your extension module. This is passed to the function as the self parameter. To find a class object you need to know which module the class is defined in. If you know this and you know that the module in question has been loaded you can retrieve the module object by name using:

- ◆ `PyObject *PyImport_AddModuleObject(PyObject *name)`
- ◆ `PyObject *PyImport_AddModule(const char *name)`

The first uses a Python string for the name of the module and the second uses a C string. Despite the name of the function, this doesn't load the module. As long as the module is loaded it returns a module object that references it and NULL otherwise.

If you want to get the main module you would use:

- ◆ `PyObject *main=PyImport_AddModule("__main__");`

Once we have a module object you can retrieve any class or module attribute using its __dict__ attribute. The simplest way to get a module's dict is:

- ◆ `PyObject *PyModule_GetDict(PyObject *module)`

which returns a dict object belonging to the module object specified. For example:

```
PyObject *maindict = PyModule_GetDict(main);
```

The dict object can be used to get a Python object for any of the module's attributes. For example, to retrieve the class object corresponding to myClass:

```
PyObject *myclass = PyDict_GetItemString(maindict, "myClass");
```

Working with dict objects is explored in a later chapter but you can see how this retrieves the value, a class object, that corresponds to the key "myClass".

With this class object we can test that another object is an instance of this or a sub-class:

```
PyObject_IsInstance(myObject, myclass)
```

Putting all this together we can test that the object has all of the attributes of myClass using:

```
static PyObject *Attributes4(PyObject *self, PyObject *args)
{
  PyObject *myObject;
  if (!PyArg_ParseTuple(args, "O", &myObject))
    return NULL;
  PyObject *main = PyImport_AddModule("__main__");
  PyObject *maindict = PyModule_GetDict(main);
  PyObject *myclass = PyDict_GetItemString(maindict, "myClass");

  if (PyObject_IsInstance(myObject, myclass))
  {
    PyObject *myAtt1 = PyObject_GetAttrString(myObject,
                                              "myAttribute1");
    if (PyLong_Check(myAtt1))
    {
      int myValue = PyLong_AsLong(myAtt1);
      printf("%d\n", myValue);
    }
    Py_XDECREF(myAtt1);
  }
  Py_RETURN_NONE;

}
```

Notice that we have to decrement the reference count of myAtt1, but only if it is actually created. Keeping track of references is tricky. If you try this out you will find that it displays myAtt1 only if you pass it an instance of myClass and only if it is currently a Python integer.

A complete listing of all of the functions given in this chapter, together with test Python code can be found on the book's webpage at www.iopress.info.

Summary

- `PyArg_ParseTuple` can return a pointer to a general Python object using the "O" format

- The simplest form of garbage collection implemented in Python is reference counting. Each time a reference is created the count is incremented and when a reference is lost it is decremented.

- When the reference count is zero the object is not accessible from Python and so the memory it uses is freed.

- Reference counting has to be supplemented by cyclic reference detection but keeping accurate reference counts is a prerequisite for correct garbage collection.

- C programs can create, set, get and delete object attributes using a range of simple function calls.

- Working with attributes usually involves converting Python objects to C objects and vice versa. There is a range of functions for standard conversions.

- Converting numeric values is easy as long as the range covered is taken into account.

- String conversion is difficult because of the use of different encodings, but the most common functions work with C strings coded as UTF-8.

- Setting and getting attributes is easy, but you need to keep the reference count correct.

- One way of checking that an object has a set of attributes is to test its type.

Chapter 8

More Complex Objects – Tuples, Lists and Dicts

Once you have the basic idea of converting simple data types between Python and C, it all seems straightforward. Converting more complex data structures such as tuples, lists and dicts is much more challenging as C doesn't have these structures as native data types.

Tuples, Lists and Dicts

Lists and tuples are examples of sequences and iterables and there are also functions that let you work with these more general categories of object, but tuples and lists are so common there are special functions that work just with them.

We have already discovered a way to extract values from a tuple/list and construct a new tuple/list/dict using Py_BuildValue. This approach makes use of lower-level functions that allow you to create a new tuple/list object and access the elements of a tuple/list.

To create a tuple, list or dict:

- PyObject *PyTuple_New(Py_ssize_t len)
- PyObject *PyList_New(Py_ssize_t len)
- PyObject *PyDict_New()

In each cases the object is empty, i.e. it doesn't have any elements and it has storage for len elements. As each element is a pointer to an element they are initialized to NULL.

A tuple is supposed to be immutable in Python, but this is not enforced in C. You can set the elements of a tuple and even resize the tuple:

- int _PyTuple_Resize(PyObject **p, Py_ssize_t newsize)

Following this the tuple will be larger or smaller and the new elements will point to NULL. Obviously, this isn't a good idea if the tuple is already in use by Python code, which expects it to be immutable. It is best avoided, but it can be useful if your function is generating a new tuple and isn't sure of its final size.

A list is mutable and you can change the size of the list by inserting or appending new elements.

If you need to know the current size of a tuple, list or dict you can use:

- ◆ `Py_ssize_t PyTuple_Size(PyObject *p)`
- ◆ `Py_ssize_t PyTuple_GET_SIZE(PyObject *p)`
- ◆ `Py_ssize_t PyList_Size(PyObject *list)`
- ◆ `Py_ssize_t PyList_GET_SIZE(PyObject *list)`
- ◆ `Py_ssize_t PyDict_Size(PyObject *p)`

The `GET_SIZE` versions of the functions return the size with no error checking.

You can test to see if an object is a tuple, list or dict:

- ◆ `int PyTuple_Check(PyObject *p)`
- ◆ `int PyTuple_CheckExact(PyObject *p)`
- ◆ `int PyList_Check(PyObject *p)`
- ◆ `int PyList_CheckExact(PyObject *p)`
- ◆ `int PyDict_Check(PyObject *p)`
- ◆ `int PyDict_CheckExact(PyObject *p)`

As always, the functions return `True` if the object is an instance of the type or subtype and the `Exact` functions only return `True` for an instance.

Finally you can convert a list to a tuple:

- ◆ `PyObject *PyList_AsTuple(PyObject *list)`

but there is no supplied function that converts a tuple to a list.

You can convert a dict into a list of items, keys or values:

- ◆ `PyObject *PyDict_Items(PyObject *p)`
- ◆ `PyObject *PyDict_Keys(PyObject *p)`
- ◆ `PyObject *PyDict_Values(PyObject *p)`

Each of these return a new object with a reference count of one.

Setting Tuple and List Elements

To set an element in a tuple or a list you use:

- ◆ `int PyTuple_SetItem(PyObject *tuple, Py_ssize_t index,`
  `                                      PyObject *item)`
- ◆ `int PyList_SetItem(PyObject *list, Py_ssize_t index,`
  `                                    PyObject *item)`

Both of these will decrement the reference count of the object already referenced at the `index` but they do not increment the reference count of the `item`. What this means is that you can create a new object with a reference count of one and set it into a tuple or a list and it will still have a reference count of one and the item it replaces will have its count reduced by one. Not incrementing the reference count is called stealing a reference because we now have an item and the element both referencing the new object, but the reference count is still just one. Of course, item is just a C variable and so it doesn't contribute to the reference count unless it persists after the C function has finished.

For example to create a tuple with integer values:

```
static PyObject *tuple1(PyObject *self, PyObject *args)
{
  PyObject *myTuple = PyTuple_New(10);
  for (int i = 0; i < 10; i++)
  {
    PyObject *item = PyLong_FromLong(i);
    PyTuple_SetItem(myTuple, i, item);
  }
  return myTuple;
}
```

Notice that there is no need to decrement the reference count of item as this is stolen by the element of the tuple

If you try this out:

```
import example
print(example.tuple1())
```

you will see:

```
(0, 1, 2, 3, 4, 5, 6, 7, 8, 9)
```

Notice that even in C a Python tuple is supposed to be immutable and to reflect this the more general PyObject_SetItem() and PySequence_SetItem() functions do not work with a tuple. You are advised to use Py_Tuple_SetItem only with tuples you have created, i.e. don't use it to modify tuples passed into the function.

If you change PyTuple_New to PyList_New and PyTuple_SetItem to PyList_SetItem the function will return a list initialized in the same way:

```
static PyObject *list1(PyObject *self, PyObject *args)
{
    PyObject *mylist = PyList_New(10);
    for (int i = 0; i < 10; i++)
    {
        PyObject *item = PyLong_FromLong(i);
        PyList_SetItem(mylist, i, item);
    }
    return mylist;
}
```

The tuple also has a function which both creates and initializes a tuple:

♦ PyObject *PyTuple_Pack(Py_ssize_t n, ...)

The tuple has n elements and these have to be specified by n variables pointing at PyObjects. This is equivalent to using the Py_BuildValue function. There is no equivalent function for a list, but you can still use the Py_BuildValue function.

The list does have two "set" functions that the tuple doesn't support:

- ◆ `int PyList_Insert(PyObject *list, Py_ssize_t index, PyObject *item)`
- ◆ `int PyList_Append(PyObject *list, PyObject *item)`

The `Insert` function makes the list one element larger by inserting the `item` to become the index element, i.e. `list[index]` is the new element. Inserting at `index = 0` adds item to the front of the list and `index = len(list)` adds the item to the end of the list which is what `Append` does. Both functions increment the reference count of the object being inserted or appended.

You might think that you can create a zero item list and build up what you need using append:

```
PyObject *itemlist = PyList_New(0);
PyList_Append(itemlist, PyLong_FromLong(0));
PyList_Append(itemlist, PyLong_FromLong(1));
PyList_Append(itemlist, PyLong_FromLong(2));
```

However, while this works it introduces a problem with reference counting. The object created using `PyLong_FromLong()` automatically has a reference count of one. When this is appended to the list its reference count is incremented and hence every element of the list has a reference count of two, not the count of one it should have. To correct the count you have to do something like:

```
static PyObject *list2(PyObject *self, PyObject *args)
{
    PyObject *itemlist = PyList_New(0);

    for (int i = 0; i < 10; i++)
    {
        PyObject *item = PyLong_FromLong(i);
        PyList_Append(itemlist, PyLong_FromLong(i));
        Py_DECREF(PyList_GetItem(itemlist, i));
    }
    return itemlist;
}
```

There is no simple fix for this that makes it worth using this idiom. Use either `Py_BuildValue` or `PyTuple_SetItem`/`PyList_SetItem` which leave the reference count of the element set to one.

Setting Dicts

Setting a dict element works much like the equivalent operation for a tuple or list but there are some important differences:

- ◆ int PyDict_SetItem(PyObject *dict, PyObject *key,
                                              PyObject *val)
- ◆ int PyDict_SetItemString(PyObject *dict, const char *key,
                                              PyObject *val)
- ◆ PyObject *PyDict_SetDefault(PyObject *dict, PyObject *key,
                                              PyObject *defaultobj)

The first version requires you to explicitly construct the Python objects used for the key and val and the second will use a key specified as a string. The third function will return the value if key is in the dict and otherwise it will insert key with the defaultobj as its value and return defaultobj.

Apart from having to specify a key as well as a value, the big difference is that this increments the reference count of both the key and the value, i.e. it does not steal a reference. For example:

```
static PyObject *dict1(PyObject *self, PyObject *args)
{
  PyObject *mydict = PyDict_New();
  PyObject *val = PyLong_FromLong(42);
  PyObject *key=PyUnicode_DecodeUTF8("Item0", 5, NULL);
  PyDict_SetItem(mydict, key, val);
  return mydict;
}
```

returns a dict with a single element.

The problem with this example is that both the key and the val have reference counts of two rather than one. The solution is to manually decrement their counts before returning the result:

```
static PyObject *dict1(PyObject *self, PyObject *args)
{
  PyObject *mydict = PyDict_New();
  PyObject *val = PyLong_FromLong(42);
  PyObject *key = PyUnicode_DecodeUTF8("Item0", 5, NULL);
  PyDict_SetItem(mydict, key, val);
  Py_DECREF(val);
  Py_DECREF(key);
  return mydict;
}
```

Notice that you should avoid decrementing the reference count too early. If you reduce it to zero then the objects will be garbage-collected before you have used them in the dict.

If you clear a dict using:

- `void PyDict_Clear(PyObject *dict)`

then all of the key and element objects have their reference counts decremented. Similarly deleting a single element:

- `int PyDict_DelItem(PyObject *dict, PyObject *key)`
- `int PyDict_DelItemString(PyObject *p, const char *key)`

decrements both the key and the value.

Getting Elements

To access elements you can use:

- `PyObject *PyTuple_GetItem(PyObject *tuple, Py_ssize_t index)`
- `PyObject *PyList_GetItem(PyObject *list, Py_ssize_t index)`
- `PyObject *PyDict_GetItem(PyObject *dict, PyObject *key)`
- `PyObject *PyDict_GetItemString(PyObject *dict,`
                                              `const char *key)`
- `PyObject *PyDict_GetItemWithError(PyObject *dict,`
                                          `PyObject *key)`

There are versions of the list and tuple functions with `GETITEM` in capitals that do not perform checks for errors. The `WithError` function returns `NULL` and raises an exception if the key isn't in the dict whereas the other two function simply return `NULL`.

You can use:

- `int PyDict_Contains(PyObject *dict, PyObject *key)`

to check that a key is in the dict before you try to retrieve the value.

The functions do not increment the reference count for the object that the element references – they borrow the reference. For example, if the elements of a tuple or a list are all of the same type you can use a for loop to unpack them into variables or an array:

```
static PyObject *tuple2(PyObject *self, PyObject *args)
{
    PyObject *myTuple;
    if (!PyArg_ParseTuple(args, "O", &myTuple))
        return NULL;
    int myarray[10];
    for (int i = 0; i < 10; i++)
    {
        PyObject *item = PyTuple_GetItem(myTuple, i);
        myarray[i] = PyLong_AsLong(item);
        printf("%d ", myarray[i]);
    }
    printf("\n");
    Py_RETURN_NONE;
}
```

You can use this approach as long as the elements are all of the same type, or a reasonably limited range of types for which you have conversion functions. Moving each element from a tuple or a list into an array isn't a particularly fast operation and this needs to be kept in mind when passing large tuples or lists. If you need to move large amounts of data into your C program, a bytes object, byte array, or any object that supports the buffer protocol, is a better choice.

The important point is that getting an element of a tuple, list or dict does not increment its reference count.

Slices

Both tuples and lists support slices in C, but tuples only allow you to get a slice and not set a slice – in deference to their immutability in Python.

To get a slice:

◆ PyObject *PyTuple_GetSlice(PyObject *tuple, Py_ssize_t low,
                                              Py_ssize_t high)
◆ PyObject *PyList_GetSlice(PyObject *list, Py_ssize_t low,
                                             Py_ssize_t high)

These return a new tuple or list containing the elements from low to high.

The list, but not the tuple, also supports setting a slice:

◆ int PyList_SetSlice(PyObject *list, Py_ssize_t low,
                           Py_ssize_t high, PyObject *itemlist)

This sets the slice of list between low and high to the contents of itemlist. It works by deleting the items between and including low and high and inserting however many elements are in itemList in their place. Notice that high isn't deleted. The set slice operation increments the reference count of each item in the itemList that is inserted into the list and decrements the reference count of items removed. The items already in the list retain their reference count unchanged.

The itemlist may be NULL, indicating the assignment of an empty list and this results in the slice being deleted, for example:

```
static PyObject *list3(PyObject *self, PyObject *args)
{
    PyObject *mylist;
    if (!PyArg_ParseTuple(args, "O", &mylist))
        return NULL;
    PyObject *itemlist = PyList_New(4);
    PyList_SetItem(itemlist, 0, PyLong_FromLong(10));
    PyList_SetItem(itemlist, 1, PyLong_FromLong(11));
    PyList_SetItem(itemlist, 2, PyLong_FromLong(12));
    PyList_SetItem(itemlist, 3, PyLong_FromLong(13));
    PyList_SetSlice(mylist, 3, 5, itemlist);
    Py_DECREF(itemlist);
    Py_RETURN_NONE;
}
```

Notice that after the `PyList_SetItem` each item in `itemlist` has a reference count of one. Then when the `PyList_SetSlice` is completed the elements list and `itemlist` have a reference count of two. When the reference count of `itemList` is reduced by one it becomes zero and `itemList` is garbage-collected and all of its elements have their reference count reduced by one. Thus, finally, the new elements in list have a reference count of one, which is correct.

If you try this out:

```
import example
mylist=[0,1,2,3,4,5,6,7,8,9]
example.list3(mylist))
print(myList)
```

you will see:

```
[0, 1, 2, 10, 11, 12, 13, 5, 6, 7, 8, 9]
```

Notice that elements 3 and 4 have been deleted and all of the elements in `itemList` have been inserted.

In-Place List Operations

The list also supports two in-place rearrangements. The `sort` function performs an in place sort:

◆ `int PyList_Sort(PyObject *list)`

and

◆ `int PyList_Reverse(PyObject *list)`

performs an in-place reversal of the list.

As Python's sort routine is fast it is better to sort a Python list rather than convert it to an array and then sort it. Neither operation changes the reference counts.

Sequence Protocols

Tuple and lists are the prime examples of sequence objects. A sequence object supports indexed access. That is, if `s` is a sequence object you can write things like:

```
s[i]=42
```

and

```
print(s[i])
```

A sequence object supports `__len__` and `__getitem__` and this is all that is needed to make use of index notation, as long as the permitted index runs from 0 to the length of the object. As already mentioned, lists and tuples are sequence objects as are bytes, byte arrays and strings, but dicts are not. The reason is that a dict can use non-integer keys and while a dict that uses only integer keys is a sequence object, this isn't true in general.

Notice that there is no function that will create a new sequence object within a C function. To do this you need to know how to create a general Python object. You can check to see if an object supports the sequence protocol using:

- `int PySequence_Check(PyObject *sequence)`

This returns `True` if the object has a `__getitem__` method, unless it is a subclass of `dict`. As long as it is a sequence object, you can find its length using:

- `Py_ssize_t PySequence_Size(PyObject *sequence)`
- `Py_ssize_t PySequence_Length(PyObject *sequence)`

There is no difference between the functions.

You can get an item using either:

- `PyObject *PySequence_GetItem(PyObject *sequence, Py_ssize_t index)`
- `PyObject *PySequence_ITEM(PyObject *sequence, Py_ssize_t index)`

The difference between the two is that `ITEM` doesn't check that the object is a sequence object and hence is faster.

Unlike the equivalent get functions for a tuple and a list, these functions do increment the reference count of the object returned. That is, they return a new reference not a borrowed reference. In this case you need to remember to decrement the reference count when you no longer want to use the object. If you want `PySequence_GetItem` to behave like its tuple/list equivalent use:

```
temp=PySequence_GetItem(myList,0);
Py_DECREF(temp);
```

As incrementing the reference count is the most common behavior of functions that return Python objects it is often suggested that `PySequence_GetItem` is used in preference to `PyList_GetItem` or `PyTuple_GetItem` to ensure uniformity of behavior.

The function to set an item in a sequence object is:

- `int PySequence_SetItem(PyObject *sequence, Py_ssize_t index, PyObject *item)`

Again unlike the equivalent tuple and list `SetItem` functions this function does not steal a reference from `item`, instead it increments the item's reference count.

This is an important difference. For example, following:

```
PyObject *temp=PyLong_FromLong(42);
PyList_SetItem(myList, 0,temp);
```

the object referenced by `myList[0]` and `temp` has a reference count of one, but following:

```
PyObject *temp=PyLong_FromLong(42);
PySequence_SetItem(myList, 0,temp);
```

the object referenced by `myList[0]` and `temp` has a reference count of two. If the function doesn't convert the reference from temp to a Python reference that persists after the function finishes this is an error. The solution is to decrement the reference count:

```
PyObject *temp = PyLong_FromLong(42);
PySequence_SetItem(myList, 0, temp);
Py_DECREF(temp);
```

Now the object referenced by `temp` and `myList[0]` has a reference count of one.

You can delete an item using:

- `int PySequence_DelItem(PyObject *sequence, Py_ssize_t index)`

This deletes the item at `sequence[index]` which results in the re-indexing of all of the items that follow. The reference count of the item removed is decremented and the rest of the reference counts are unchanged.

There are sequence equivalents of the tuple/list slice functions:

- `PyObject *PySequence_GetSlice(PyObject *sequence, Py_ssize_t index1, Py_ssize_t index2)`
- `int PySequence_SetSlice(PyObject *sequence, Py_ssize_t index1,Py_ssize_t index2, PyObject *v)`

and there is also a delete slice:

- `int PySequence_DelSlice(PyObject *sequence, Py_ssize_t index1, Py_ssize_t index2)`

These work in the same way and decrement the reference count of items removed and increment the reference count of items added.

You can convert a sequence object to a tuple or a list with:

- `PyObject *PySequence_Tuple(PyObject *sequence)`
- `PyObject *PySequence_List(PyObject *sequence)`

In both cases a new object, tuple, or list, is returned with reference count set to one and all of the elements in the new tuple or list reference the same objects as the original and their reference counts are unchanged.

Accessing a sequence using its __getitem__ function can be slow. You can convert a general sequence or iterable to an object that can be directly indexed without the use of __getitem__:

- PyObject *PySequence_Fast(PyObject *sequence, const char *m)

where *m* is simply the error message displayed if things go wrong.

Once you have performed the conversion you can use:

- Py_ssize_t PySequence_Fast_GET_SIZE(PyObject *fast)
- PyObject *PySequence_Fast_GET_ITEM(PyObject *fast,
                                     Py_ssize_t index)

As long as the object has been created by PySequence_Fast, the get function returns the item via a pointer to the original object. If the original object changes then the pointers are likely to be wrong, so only use this with sequences that are unmodified. The GET_ITEM function doesn't change the object reference counts.

There are also some functions that allow you to work with sequences as Python objects:

- PyObject *PySequence_Concat(PyObject *sequence1,
                             PyObject *sequence2)
- PyObject *PySequence_InPlaceConcat(PyObject *sequence1,
                                    PyObject *sequence2)
- PyObject *PySequence_Repeat(PyObject *sequence,
                             Py_ssize_t count)
- PyObject *PySequence_InPlaceRepeat(PyObject *sequence,
                                    Py_ssize_t count)

The Concat functions join the two sequences together and the Repeat functions concatenate count copies of the sequence. The InPlace functions return a reference to the modified first sequence. The functions all update the element's reference count to include the references in the new array. So for example, if you concatenate the same sequence every element's reference count would have two added to it, but if you do the concatenation in place then the count would only go up by one.

Finally there are two search function which can be useful:

- int PySequence_Contains(PyObject *sequence, PyObject *item)
- Py_ssize_t PySequence_Index(PyObject *sequence,
                             PyObject *item)

Contains returns True if the item is in the sequence and Index returns the first position of the item in the sequence or -1 if it isn't present.

Manipulating Dicts

If you want to merge two lists of tuples you can use the sequence functions, but a dict isn't regarded as a sequence hence it has its own manipulation functions:

- `int PyDict_Merge(PyObject *dict1, PyObject *dict2, int override)`
- `int PyDict_Update(PyObject *dict1, PyObject *dict2)`

the merge and update functions add key value pairs from `dict2` into `dict1`. In the case of merge, override determines what happens if the key already exists in `dict1`. If override is `True` then key value pairs overwrite any existing key value pairs in `dict1`. If it is `False` then only the new key value pairs in `dict2` are added, which is what `Update` does by default.

You can also merge a sequence of key value pairs into a dict:

- `int PyDict_MergeFromSeq2(PyObject *dict, PyObject *seq, int override)`

This works exactly like `PyDict_Merge`, but the key values are taken from a sequence. Each element of the sequence has to be a sequence with two elements, e.g. a tuple (`key,value`).

Iterator Protocol

Tuples and lists are not just sequences they both support the iterator protocol, i.e they are iterables. All that an object has to do is return an iterator object as the result of the `iter` function. An iterator object has a `__next__` method which returns the next item. If there is no next item then in Python a `StopIteration` exception is raised. In C the iterator returns a `NULL` without raising an exception.

It is tempting to think that an iterator generates a sequence of values with the first always followed by the same second and so on. This implies that the items are in some sort of order and for any integer there is an item – this is a sequence and any sequence can be iterated but not all iterators are sequences. For example, a random number iterator could return the next random number, which isn't a sequence as you get items in no particular order.

As for sequences, there is no way to create an iterator object from C. You have to know how to create a general object from a class and then add an iterator function. You can pass in an existing iterator to a function to make use of.

You can test to see if an object supports the iterator protocol:

- int PyIter_Check(PyObject *o)
- int PyAIter_Check(PyObject *o)

The first checks for a standard iterator and the second for an asynchronous iterator.

As long as the object supports an iterator you can get an iterator object using:

- PyObject *PyObject_GetIter(PyObject *o)

Once you have an iterator object you can get the next item using:

- PyObject *PyIter_Next(PyObject *iterator)

If there is no next item then a NULL is returned and if there is an error NULL is returned and an exception is set. Each time you use Next the reference count of the object returned is incremented.

The simplest example of using an iterator is:

```
static PyObject *listIterator(PyObject *self, PyObject *args)
{
 PyObject *mylist;
    if (!PyArg_ParseTuple(args, "O", &mylist))
        return NULL;

    PyObject *myIter = PyObject_GetIter(mylist);
    printf("%d ", PyLong_AsLong((PyIter_Next(myIter))));
    printf("%d ", PyLong_AsLong((PyIter_Next(myIter))));
    printf("%d ", PyLong_AsLong((PyIter_Next(myIter))));
    printf("%d ", PyLong_AsLong((PyIter_Next(myIter))));
    printf("\n");
    Py_DECREF(myIter);
    Py_RETURN_NONE;
}
```

This simply gets an iterator and then uses it to return four next items which are assumed to be integers. Notice that this approach leaves the reference count of the first four items in the iterator with a reference count incremented by one. This is probably not what is intended and the counts should be decremented before the function ends.

If you try this out:

```
import example
mylist=[0,1,2,3,4,5,6,7,8,9]
example.listIterator(mylist)
```

you will see:

0 1 2 3

A more interesting example is creating a `for in` loop:

```c
static PyObject *listFor(PyObject *self, PyObject *args)
{
  PyObject *myList;
  if (!PyArg_ParseTuple(args, "O", &myList))
    return NULL;
  PyObject *myIter = PyObject_GetIter(myList);
  for (PyObject *item = PyIter_Next(myIter);
                      item != NULL; item = PyIter_Next(myIter))
  {
    printf("%d ", PyLong_AsLong(item));
    Py_DECREF(item);
  }
  Py_DECREF(myIter);
  Py_RETURN_NONE;
}
```

The C for loop is this flexible, but it might be better to implement the loop as a `while` loop:

```c
static PyObject *listWhile(PyObject *self, PyObject *args)
{
    PyObject *myList;
    if (!PyArg_ParseTuple(args, "O", &myList))
        return NULL;
    PyObject *myIter = PyObject_GetIter(myList);
    PyObject *item;
    while (item = PyIter_Next(myIter))
    {
        printf("%d ", PyLong_AsLong(item));
        Py_DECREF(item);
    }
    Py_DECREF(myIter);
    printf("\n");
    Py_DECREF(myIter);
    Py_RETURN_NONE;
}
```

which is easier to understand. Notice that in both loops we decrement the reference count as we are not making any permanent Python references to the elements and we have to decrement the iterator object.

Iterating Dicts

Although a dict is not an iterable, it can be iterated. There is a special function that will return the key value pairs from a dict:

```
int PyDict_Next(PyObject *dict, Py_ssize_t *ppos, PyObject **pkey,
                                                  PyObject **pvalue)
```

This will return a key value pair in `pkey` and `pvalue` each time it is called. Either can be `NULL` if you don't want the corresponding item. The `ppos` variable should be set to zero before the first call and it should not be changed thereafter as it is used to keep track of the state of the iteration. The function returns `False` when there are no more elements. The reference counts of the keys and the values that are returned are not incremented, i.e. they are borrowed.

Summary

- When we move beyond simple data types that have direct C equivalents, things become more complicated.

- The Python container types, list, tuple, string and dict, are often worked with as Python objects within the C program.

- You can create list, tuple and dict objects within a C program and add other objects to them as elements.

- The tuple is supposed to be immutable, but C isn't particularly disciplined about this and you can modify a tuple.

- Getting elements is also possible, but notice that this does not change the reference count.

- Slices are supported in C but tuples, being immutable, only let you get a slice.

- You can also sort and reverse a list without creating a copy.

- The operations on lists and tuples extend to objects that implement the sequence protocol.

- Sequences support getting and setting elements and slices.

- Iterables don't have to be sequences, but they often are. An iterable provides an iterator object which can be called to get the next element.

- You can use an iterator to implement a `for` in loop or a `while` loop within a C program.

Chapter 9

Errors, Exceptions And Reference Counting

Once you start using more complex objects you are likely to need to test for conditions like an object having or not having an attribute. You may well have to pass the error back to Python or raise an error condition on your own account. Python implements a sophisticated system of exceptions which make error handling more capable than simply having to give up and post an error code.

In addition, we have to look at ways of checking that our reference counting is working if we want to avoid memory leaks and generating unexpected exceptions.

Exceptions - The Python View

Python implements exceptions to deal with runtime errors. C programmers might not be familiar with the idea of an exception. In C you generally deal with an error by setting an error code, and if you are lucky an error message, and terminating the program. More sophisticated programming languages, such as Python, implement exceptions as a way of avoiding having to terminate the program.

In Python you can write:

```
try:
    block of code
except
    error handling code
```

If any instructions in the block of code cannot be completed for any reason an exception is raised and the except clause is activated. This sounds like nothing more sophisticated than an if *error* then *handle error* construct, but it is much more. The block of code may call functions and if an exception is raised in one of the functions we have the problem of how to get back to the calling code. What happens is that the call stack is "unwound". It is as if each function in the call chain is forced to do a return with the extra step of erasing of any return values. What this means is that the effects of any function are obliterated as far as possible and the code in the except clause can run as if the block of code was never even attempted.

Of course, this doesn't erase any non-local side effects of the function. For example if the function printed something, opened a file or modified a global variable then these things are not automatically undone by the exception.

For example:

```
total=0

def myFunc(x,y):
    global total
    total=total+1
    print("in myFunc")
    ans=x/y
    return ans

try:
    myFunc(1,0)
except:
    print("Can't divide by zero")
print(total)
```

If you try this out you will see the error message, but you will also see the result of the print and total will still be incremented. Notice that the exception occurs at ans=x/y and no instructions after this are executed.

As the exception unwinds the call stack it is as if the function was never called. For example, if you add:

```
print(result)
```

at the end of the program you will see a runtime error that result doesn't exist. In principle you can try to call he function again after putting things right. The main purpose of the except clause is to allow you to undo any global changes that the function may have made and to call the function again. For example:

```
total=0
def myFunc(x,y):
    global total
    total=total+1
    print("in myFunc")
    ans=x/y
    return ans

try:
    result=myFunc(1,0)
except:
    print("Can't divide by zero")
    total=total-1
    result=myFunc(1,1)
print(result)
print(total)
```

In this case the except decrements total before calling the function again. Notice that now result exists, even if there is an exception. In general, the except clause should undo global changes including closing files, erasing data and so on.

The try/except will respond to any relevant exception from any function called within the try clause.

There may well be a chain of functions called and if one of them raises an exception then its stack frame is removed and the function that called it is examined for a try/except call. If one isn't found then the next function in the call chain is examined for a try/except. This carries on until a function with try/except is found or there are no more to examine, in which case a runtime error occurs.

Exception Classes

As the chain of functions could fail for a wide range of reasons the cause of the exception is signaled by passing an exception object which has properties that define the exception back up the function chain. The except clause can specify what exception objects it can handle. An except clause that can handle a given exception class will also handle all the derived exception objects.

The key idea is that an exception class is defined to handle a particular type of error. When an error occurs and the exception is raised, the system creates an instance of the class which is passed to any exception handlers. The exception handlers can specify the classes that they can handle.

For example, ArithmeticError is designed to be raised for any problem with arithmetic, but it also has three derived classes FloatingPointError, OverflowError and ZeroDivisionError which are actually raised when the specific problem occurs. If you want to handle all three derived cases you can specify ArithmeticError using:

```
except ArithmeticError:
```

which is called for any of FloatingPointError, OverflowError and ZeroDivisionError. If you just want to respond to a division-by-zero error you can use:

```
except ZeroDivisionError:
```

You can also specify multiple except clauses to deal with different types of exception. If you need to move outside of the exception hierarchy then you can form a group of unrelated exceptions via:

- exception ExceptionGroup(msg, excs)
- exception BaseExceptionGroup(msg, excs)

You can also get access to the exception object using as:

- except ArthmeticError as err

where the exception object has the error message and other details as attributes.

Finally, to raise an exception you use the `raise` keyword with one of the built-in exception classes, for example:

```
raise ArithmeticError
```

If you want to create your own exception class then you simply inherit from the `Exception` class or one of its derived built-in classes. You can add attributes to the new exception class that provides more information, for example:

```
class MyNumberError(ArithmeticError):
    def __init__(self, message,):
        super(MyNumberError, self).__init__(message)
```

If you now raise this exception:

```
raise MyNumberError("Number not 42")
```

and don't handle the exception then you will see the error:

```
MyNumberError: Number not 42
```

There are many more small details about Python's exception handling. For example, you can unhandle an exception by using `raise` within a handler. This reactivates the exception and passes it up to the next level.

As well as full exceptions there are also warnings which work in roughly the same way but only display the warning message and don't stop the program if they are unhandled. You can set filters to suppress warning errors.

Python Exceptions In C

As long as you understand Python exceptions, you should have no problem with supporting them within your C extensions. All of the C API functions make use of the Python exception system. If an error occurs they return either NULL if a pointer is usually returned or -1 if an int is usually returned. The PyArg_ function differ from this and return 1 for success and 0 for failure. This indicates that an error has occurred but the function also sets three pointers that define the exception.

If your C extension function returns `NULL` or `-1` without setting an exception then you will see the Python error message:

```
SystemError: <built-in function exampleFunction>
            returned NULL without setting an exception
```

A function returning an error from the C API has not only to return a `NULL` or `-1`, but also set an exception.

If you call a C API function and it returns an error you have the choice of handling the exception or returning it and allowing the Python system to try to find an exception handler. The simplest thing to do is pass the exception to the Python system. Often this means doing nothing at all. For example:

```
static PyObject* exception1(PyObject *self, PyObject *args)
{
    PyObject *x = PyLong_FromLong(1);
    PyObject *y = PyLong_FromLong(0);
    PyObject *ans =PyNumber_TrueDivide(x, y);
    Py_DECREF(x);
    Py_DECREF(y);
    return ans;
}
```

This function attempts to use `TrueDivide` to implement an integer division but the function raises a division-by-zero exception and passes back a `NULL` to indicate that there is an error. The function simply returns the result, a `NULL`, and the Python system processes the exception. Of course, you might well have to test for the `NULL` and return early, but generally you don't have to do any more. You do have to make sure that you clean up any resources used if you do return early, for example:

```
static PyObject *exception1(PyObject *self, PyObject *args)
{
    PyObject *x = PyLong_FromLong(1);
    PyObject *y = PyLong_FromLong(0);
    PyObject *ans = PyNumber_TrueDivide(x, y);
    if (ans == NULL)
    {
        Py_DECREF(x);
        Py_DECREF(y);
        return NULL;
    }
    PyObject *z = PyLong_FromLong(1);
    PyObject *ans2 = PyNumber_TrueDivide(x, z);
    Py_DECREF(x);
    Py_DECREF(y);
    Py_DECREF(z);
    return ans;
}
```

There is argument for explicitly passing a `NULL` in the return to make it clear that this is an error return.

Raising Exceptions

As well as passing exceptions raised by other functions back to the Python system, you can also quite easily raise exceptions directly using;

```
void PyErr_SetString(PyObject *type, const char *message)
```

where type is one of the standard exceptions with names starting PyExc_, such as PyExc_ZeroDivisionError and message is a UTF-8 C string that specifies the error message. For example, we can raise our own division-by-zero exception using:

```
static PyObject *exception2(PyObject *self, PyObject *args)
{
    PyErr_SetString(PyExc_ZeroDivisionError,
                        "A Dummy divide error has occurred");
    return NULL;
}
```

If you compile his and try it out:

```
import example
try:
 ans=example.exception2()
except ZeroDivisionError as err:
 print(err)
```

you will see:

```
A Dummy divide error has occurred
```

You can raise any of the builtin exceptions and warnings in the same way. You can also create your own exception classes by inheriting from Exception. Creating classes and inheritance is covered in Chapters 11 and 12 but it is very straight forward. However there is a shortcut in the form of the

```
PyObject *PyErr_NewException(const char *name,
                            PyObject *base, PyObject *dict)
```

The second and third parameters are usually set to NULL to accept the default base class, Exception, and dict. A new class is created and this can be added to the module and used in the same way as a built in exception class.

For example:

```
static PyObject *myCustomException;
PyMODINIT_FUNC PyInit_example(void)
{
    PyObject *m;
    m = PyModule_Create(&addmodule);
    if (m == NULL)
        return NULL;
    myCustomException = PyErr_NewException(
                    "example.myCustomException", NULL, NULL);
    if (PyModule_AddObjectRef(m, "myCustomException",
                                        myCustomException) < 0)
    {
        Py_CLEAR(myCustomException);
        Py_DECREF(m);
        return NULL;
    }
    return m;
}
```

This adds a new class to the module and uses the technique for adding
attributes to a module described in detail in Chapter 11. All you need to
understand at this stage is that we have created a new exception class called
myCustomException and stored it in a global variable of the same name and
added it as an attribute to the module. Notice that the adding the attribute to
the module is also an example of passing an exception up to the Python
system. The new exception class can be used by the C extension module
and Python programs that import it. For example:

```
static PyObject *exception3(PyObject *self, PyObject *args)
{
    PyErr_SetString(myCustomException,
                        "A Custom error has occurred");
    return NULL;
}
```

This raises the new exception with a suitable error message. A Python
program that makes use of this function and the new exception is:

```
try:
    ans=example.exception3()
except example.myCustomException as err:
    print(err)
```

The result is:

```
A Custom error has occurred
```

There is also a range of API functions designed to make it easier to raise
common errors.

Handling Exceptions

In most cases you are probably going to pass the exception on to the Python system but you can handle it in the C function if you can. If you handle the exception then you have to clean up anything that the function that raised the exception created before clearing the error using:

```
void PyErr_Clear()
```

Don't clear the error unless you have cleaned up after the function that raised it. Of course if you are calling a C function you can deal with any errors it returns in the usual way – you don't need to worry about Python exceptions unless you want to raise one to signal the error to the Python system.

Handling an exception can be as easy as calling `PyErr_Clear` for example:

```
static PyObject *exception3(PyObject *self, PyObject *args)
{
    PyObject *x = PyLong_FromLong(1);
    PyObject *y = PyLong_FromLong(0);
    PyObject *ans = PyNumber_TrueDivide(x, y);
    if (ans == NULL)
    {   PyErr_Clear();
        PyObject *z = PyLong_FromLong(1);
        ans = PyNumber_TrueDivide(x, z);
        Py_DECREF(z);
    }
    Py_DECREF(x);
    Py_DECREF(y);
    return ans;
}
```

In this case all we have to do is test for the error, clear the exception and try again.

What if you only want to handle particular types of exception? There are two functions that can help with this:

- `int PyErr_ExceptionMatches(PyObject *exc)`
- `int PyErr_GivenExceptionMatches(PyObject *given, PyObject *exc)`

The first tests to see if the current exception matches `exc`, i.e. is an instance or a derived type. If `exc` is a tuple all classes are tested. The given parameter specifies a class to compare `exc` to. `PyErr_ExceptionMatches` should only be called when an exception is actually raised. You can discover if an exception is raised using:

- `PyObject *PyErr_Occurred()`

It returns NULL if there is no exception or the exception object without incrementing its reference count. For example, to test specifically for division by zero and only handling the exception if it is:

```
static PyObject *exception5(PyObject *self, PyObject *args)
{
     PyObject *x = PyLong_FromLong(1);
     PyObject *y = PyLong_FromLong(0);
     PyObject *ans = PyNumber_TrueDivide(x, y);

     if (PyErr_Occurred() != NULL)
     {
          if(PyErr_ExceptionMatches(PyExc_ZeroDivisionError)){
               PyErr_Clear();
               PyObject *z = PyLong_FromLong(1);
               ans = PyNumber_TrueDivide(x, z);
               Py_DECREF(z);
          }
     }
     Py_DECREF(x);
     Py_DECREF(y);
     return ans;
}
```

Notice that if the exception is anything except a division-by zero-error it is passed back to the Python system.

Testing Reference Counting

One of the most common causes of errors and exceptions is reference counting. Reference counting is at its most complex when you are working with containers like tuples, lists, sequences and dicts. There are times when you just need to check that the reference count is what you expect it to be. In principle this is easy, but in practice there are some complications.

The key to finding out about reference counts in C is the Py_REFCNT macro. If you want to know the reference count of the object referenced by temp you would use:

```
printf("ref count= %lld\n", Py_REFCNT(temp));
```

Notice that it is the object that keeps the reference count, not the variable. You can have multiple variables referencing the same object and they will all return the same reference count. For example:

```
printf("ref count= %lld\n", Py_REFCNT(temp));
temp2=temp;
printf("ref count= %lld\n", Py_REFCNT(temp2));
```

displays the same reference count – this is just a result of the fact that Python "knows" nothing about what you are doing in C. Notice that this isn't necessarily true if you obtain the reference via a container, for example:

```
PyObject *temp=PySequence_GetItem(myList,0);
printf("ref count= %lld\n", Py_REFCNT(temp));
PyObject *temp2=PySequence_GetItem(myList,0);
printf("ref count= %lld\n", Py_REFCNT(temp2));
```

Now the reference count is incremented by the first `GetItem` and again by the second – i.e. the act of getting a reference to the object changes the reference count. As already discussed, this isn't always the case as `PyList_GetItem` and `PyTuple_GetItem` don't increment the reference count. If you are in any doubt and need proof of what is going on, get the reference twice and see if the reference count stays the same or increments.

For objects that you create within the C function you can work out what the final reference count should be. If you are returning a Python object then it should have reference count of one. If you are discarding a Python object then it should have a reference count of zero. You can check these assertions using the `Py_REFCNT` macro at the end of the function.

An Example

If you pass in a primitive Python object for the C function to work with then you will discover that its reference count isn't what you might think it is by working it out. For example, what do you think the reference count for the first element of the list is:

```
myList = [0,1,2,3,4,5,6,7,8,9]
```

The naive answer is one as the zero object is only referenced by `myList`. If you check its reference count within the C function you will discover that it is a very big number. The reason is that many primitive data types are cached and the cached object is referenced from many places in the Python interpreter. All of the integers from -5 to 256 are in the cache as soon as the Python interpreter starts to save the time needed to create them. This makes them difficult to use for checking reference counts. If you want to have a "clean" example without the cache getting in the way you have to use a numeric value or string that hasn't been used in the system, for example:

```
myList = [257,1,2,3,4,5,6,7,8,9]
```

In this case the reference count for the first element is two which is more reasonable, but not the one you might expect. The other two references are internal to the Python interpreter.

What all this means is that the C function should not set the reference count of a passed-in object to one, even if this is what you work out it should be in terms of the references that you have determined it to have. Instead, you should increment its reference count for each new Python reference you have created.

To check that you have done things correctly, you need to discover the reference count when the object is passed into the C function and check its value against the reference count when the C function ends. For example:

```
static PyObject *list1(PyObject *self, PyObject *args)
{
  PyObject *myList;
  if (!PyArg_ParseTuple(args, "O", &myList))
    return NULL;
  printf("myList %ld\n", Py_REFCNT(myList));
  PyObject *temp = PyList_GetItem(myList, 0);
  printf("item zero %ld\n", Py_REFCNT(temp));
  PyObject *myList2 = PySequence_InPlaceConcat(myList, myList);
  temp = PyList_GetItem(myList, 0);
  printf("myList %ld\n", Py_REFCNT(myList));
  printf("item zero %ld\n", Py_REFCNT(temp));
  Py_RETURN_NONE;
}
```

When used by:

```
myList=[257,1,2,3,4,5,6,7,8,9]
example.list1(myList)
```

it displays:

```
myList 3
item zero 3
myList 4
item zero 4
```

You can see that the list that is passed in starts with a reference count of three but at the end of the function it has a reference count of four. This isn't correct as no new Python references have been created, i.e. it isn't returned by the function and the reference from myList2 is lost. This suggests that we need to add:

```
Py_DECREF(myList);
```

but this is wrong as an analysis gives:

PyArg_ParseTuple O	adds a reference to myList
PyList_GetItem	borrows a reference to element zero
PySequence_InPlaceConcat	adds a reference to myList
	it also adds a new reference to each element added to myList.

For example, the object referenced by element zero is now referenced by PyList_GetItem which borrows a reference to element zero

So `myList` has its reference count incremented by 2 not 1. The error is caused by not knowing the reference count of the list object until it has been converted by `PyArg_ParseTuple`. As a result we need:

```
Py_DECREF(myList);
Py_DECREF(myList);
```

to make the reference count correct.

Similarly element zero initially has a reference count of three and ends the function with a count of four. This is appropriate as the list now references it twice once in its original location, element zero and once more as element 10. Thus the object referenced by element zero has had its reference count incremented by one. This is correct and we don't need to modify the count.

This is typical of an investigation into reference counts. You first gather some data and then check that it corresponds with what you expect. Then you add increments and decrements to set the counts to what they should be.

Using sys and gc

On the Python side of the program we can use `sys.getrefcount(object)`. For example:

```
print("ref count=",sys.getrefcount(myList[0])-1)
example.list2(myList)
print("ref count=",sys.getrefcount(myList[0])-1)
```

indicates that the reference count of the first element is three before the call and four after.

You can also use:

```
gc.collect()
```

to force a garbage collection to make sure that all of the references are live before you examine the reference counts.

The gc function `get_objects` returns a list of all of the objects currently being tracked, but this is a much longer list than you might expect:

```
print(gc.get_objects())
```

It is also sometimes useful to check that a custom object is actually garbage-collected when its reference count should be zero by defining its __del__ destructor method. This is called by the garbage collector at an undefined point in the object's destruction and you can use it to print a message that the object is indeed no more, and has ceased to be...

Summary

- C doesn't provide any error handling beyond error numbers and error messages and most often an error means a runtime error.

- Python provides a sophisticated exception system designed to allow errors to be caught and corrected, so avoiding a runtime error.

- An exception is raised by the system creating an instance of an exception class and then moving up the call stack to find the first try/except that will handle the exception.

- If no try/except is found then a runtime error occurs.

- A `try` clause can be set to accept specific exceptions by specifying the classes and hence derived objects it can handle.

- A Python program can raise a built-in exception using the `raise` keyword and it can raise a custom exception by inheriting from the `Exception` base class.

- A Python C function returns `NULL` or `-1` to signal that an error has occurred and sets three system variable to specify the exception.

- Returning `NULL` or `-1` without raising an exception is a run time error.

- The C API provides a range of classes that represent built-in exceptions and you can create derived classes to represent custom exceptions.

- The C API can raise an exception by creating an exception object and returning `NULL` or `-1`.

- In most cases a C function will pass on any error that a C API function returns to the system after doing any cleaning up that might be necessary.

- A C function can also test for the type of exception and handle it if this is possible.

- Reference counting is very difficult to get right and is the cause of many errors and exceptions.

- You can discover what the reference count is in C and Python.

- Objects passed into a C function may not have the reference count you expect due to system references and caching. Check that the change in the reference count is correct.

- You can use the `sys` and `gc` modules to monitor and control garbage collection.

Chapter 10

Bytes And Strings

We have already looked at the basics of working with strings, but there is a lot more to find out. Python strings are not only important for Python programs, they also provide a sophisticated string handling library that can be used in C. This not only provides basic string manipulation, but it solves the problem of working with Unicode and other encodings in C. In short, it is very useful to leave Python strings unconverted and use them to do string manipulation in C.

When you have finished working with Python Unicode strings, however, there is usually a need to convert them to some other representation, either as a C string or as a Python bytes or bytearray object. To do this we need the help of encoders and decoders.

The central reason for using Python strings is that they are Unicode. In many languages strings are ASCII and as such provide an easy way to work with byte arrays. Python strings, because they do not always use one byte per character, are not so useful in this role. For this reason Python provides the bytes and bytearray objects. In many ways you can think of bytes and bytearrays as being equivalent to ASCII strings as they behave a lot like strings with ASCII encoding. As C strings are by default ASCII-encoded they are a natural match for bytes and bytearrays.

Bytes and Bytearray

The bytearray is a mutable sequence of elements that are bytes. The bytes object is its immutable counterpart. They both work in much the same way with the exception of any operations which would attempt to modify the immutable bytes object. As they are both sequences and iterables you can use all of the functions introduced in Chapter 8 for these two protocols.

You can test for an object of the type using:

- ◆ `int PyBytes_Check(PyObject *o)`
- ◆ `int PyBytes_CheckExact(PyObject *o)`
- ◆ `int PyByteArray_Check(PyObject *o)`
- ◆ `int PyByteArray_CheckExact(PyObject *o)`

The Exact versions only return True if the object is bytes or bytearray and not an instance of a subclass.

There are no functions to create an uninitialized bytes or bytearray.

To find the current size use:

- `Py_ssize_t PyBytes_Size(PyObject *o)`
- `Py_ssize_t PyBytes_GET_SIZE(PyObject *o)`
- `Py_ssize_t PyByteArray_Size(PyObject *bytearray)`
- `Py_ssize_t PyByteArray_GET_SIZE(PyObject *bytearray)`

As before the `GET_SIZE` functions don't do any error checking.

You have to create both bytes and bytearray objects from C data. The bytes object has three functions that convert C data:

- `PyObject *PyBytes_FromString(const char *v)`
- `PyObject *PyBytes_FromStringAndSize(const char *v,`
  `                                          Py_ssize_t len)`
- `PyObject *PyBytes_FromFormat(const char *format, ...)`

Each sets the reference count of bytes to one. The `FromFormat` version uses a subset of the same format specifiers that `printf` uses:

Format	Type
%%	Escape for %
%c	`int`
%d	`int`
%u	`unsigned int`
%ld	`long`
%lu	`unsigned long`
%zd	`Py_ssize_t`
%zu	`size_t`
%i	`int`
%x	`int`
%s	`const char*`
%p	`const void*`

The key idea here is that the bytes that represent the C data type are converted to ASCII/UTF-8 in the same way that they would be using a `printf`. For example:

`PyObject *myBytes2= PyBytes_FromFormat("%x", 15);`

returns the ASCII/UTF8 code for "f".

The bytearray only provides a single function to create a bytearray:

- `PyObject *PyByteArray_FromStringAndSize(const char *string, Py_ssize_t len)`

There is also a pair of functions which will convert a general object that supports the buffer protocol to a bytes or bytearray:

- `PyObject *PyBytes_FromObject(PyObject *o)`
- `PyObject *PyByteArray_FromObject(PyObject *o)`

The return value is a Pbuffer object which gives access to the data stored in the bytes or bytearray.

Going the other way we can convert a bytes or bytearray to a C string:

- `char *PyBytes_AsString(PyObject *o)`
- `char *PyBytes_AS_STRING(PyObject *string)`
- `char *PyByteArray_AsString(PyObject *bytearray)`
- `char *PyByteArray_AS_STRING(PyObject *bytearray)`

The functions with AS_STRING do the same job, but without error checking for a NULL pointer. All of them return a pointer to an internal buffer – they do not make a copy of the data contained in the bytes or bytearray object. You should not try to change the buffer of a byte object – it is supposed to be immutable but you can modify the buffer of a bytearray.

The bytes object has an additional function:

```
int PyBytes_AsStringAndSize(PyObject *obj, char **buffer,
                                          Py_ssize_t *length)
```

The buffer is NULL terminated and may contain NULLs if the *length is not NULL when the length of the string is returned in length. The buffer is internal to the bytes object and must not be changed. For example:

```
static PyObject *bytes1(PyObject *self, PyObject *args)
{
  char *myString="Hello World";
  PyObject *myBytes=PyBytes_FromString(myString);
  return myBytes;
}
```

simply returns the byte sequence that represents "Hello World" in ASCII.

If you try it out:

```
mybytes=example.bytes1()
print(mybytes)
```

you will see:

```
b'Hello World'
```

The leading b signifies a bytes literal which is printed using ASCII where possible. As you can see the bytes object is treated much like an ASCII string. If you go beyond the basic 0 to 127 ASCII range then the values are represented in Python by hex values.

Notice that both `bytes` and `bytearray` are sequences and iterables and you can use slicing, get and set and so on. However, if you try to modify a bytes object using a sequence function you will find that it refuses to do it, honoring the immutability in Python.

If you want to modify the data in a bytes object you have to first convert it to a bytesarray object. There is no simple function that will do this, but you can use:

```
PyObject *myByteArray = PyByteArray_FromStringAndSize(
            PyBytes_AsString(myBytes), PyBytes_Size(myBytes));
```

This first gets a pointer to the internal string buffer in `myBytes` and uses it to create a new `bytearray`. Notice that this copies the contents of the buffer to that of the new `bytearray` – this is unavoidable as you want to modify the data. Now we can use the slice functions:

```
 char *HelloMessage = "Hello World";
 PyObject *insert = PyByteArray_FromStringAndSize(
                            HelloMessage, strlen(HelloMessage));
 PySequence_SetSlice(myByteArray, 3, 7, insert);
return myByteArray;
```

The complete `bytes2` function is:

```
static PyObject *bytes2(PyObject *self, PyObject *args)
{
     PyObject *myBytes;
     if (!PyArg_ParseTuple(args, "O", &myBytes))
          return NULL;

     Py_ssize_t len = PyBytes_Size(myBytes);
     for (int i = 1; i < len; i++)
     {
          PyObject *item = PySequence_GetItem(myBytes, i);
          char c = (char)PyLong_AsLong(item);
          printf("%X  ", c);
     }
     printf("\n");
     PyObject *myByteArray = PyByteArray_FromStringAndSize(
          PyBytes_AsString(myBytes), PyBytes_Size(myBytes));

     char *HelloMessage = "Hello World";
     PyObject *insert = PyByteArray_FromStringAndSize(
                            HelloMessage, strlen(HelloMessage));

     PySequence_SetSlice(myByteArray, 3, 7, insert);
     return myByteArray;
}
```

If you try this out:

```
mybytes=example.bytes2(b"My long message")
print()
print(mybytes)
```

the result is:

```
79  20  6C  6F  6E  67  20  6D  65  73  73  61  67  65
bytearray(b'My Hello World message')
```

You can achieve most of what you need using `bytes` and `bytearray` along with sequence and iterator functions.

Python Strings

We have already discovered that Python strings are sequences and iterables, but they are also immutable. When you modify a string in Python a completely new string is created. In Python 3 a str is a Unicode object.

The most important thing to know is that Python strings are not encoded – they store the Unicode code point for each character. To do this in a space-saving way without the use of an encoding, the number of bytes used per character is variable – it can be one, two or four and this is referred to as its "kind".

If you select a Unicode object that allocates one byte per element, a `PyUnicode_1BYTE_KIND,` then you can only represent characters up to code point 255 – this is extended ASCII. If you select a Unicode object that has two bytes per element, `PyUnicode_2BYTE_KIND` then you can represent up to code point 65535, which is called the Basic Multilingual Plane or BMP. This contains most of the important characters for almost all modern languages. If the Unicode object has four bytes per element, a `PyUnicode_4BYTE_KIND,` then it can represent the entire Unicode range to code point 1114111.

It is important to understand that a Unicode object doesn't encode the code point. If the code point is stored in a single byte then this is the first byte of a 21-bit value with all other bits assumed to be zero. If the code point is stored in two bytes then these are the first two bytes of a 21-bit value with all other bits assumed zero and so on.

When a Python string is created, the smallest storage unit that can represent the code points is selected – that is the kind of string use depends on how it is initialized. For example when you use:

```
s="My long message"
```

then, as each character in the literal can be represented by code points below 255, a single-byte element string is created.

If you use:

```
s="My long message \uCE94"
```

then two bytes are allocated to store each character. Finally if you use:

```
s="My long message \U0001F600"
```

then four bytes are allocated to store each character. In each case the type of s is str which is a Unicode object of the particular kind. The terms Python string, str and Unicode object are interchangeable in Python 3.

A string will always use the number of bytes per element needed to store its largest code point. If you manipulate and combine strings then the result is a new string which, once again, has the number of bytes per element needed to store the largest code point in the result.

For completeness, there is also a variation on the PyUnicode_1BYTE_KIND that you need to be aware of. Unicode objects that are marked as ASCII strings have code points below 128 and use a single byte per character.

Unicode Strings

Within the C API a Unicode string, i.e. a Python str, is referred to as a Unicode object and all of the functions are prefaced by PyUnicode.

You can test to see if an object is a Python string using:

- int PyUnicode_Check(PyObject *o)
- int PyUnicode_CheckExact(PyObject *o)

The Exact version returns False if the object is a subtype of str.

Usually you can ignore the kind of a Unicode string, i.e. how many bytes are used to store it, as the C API functions take care of things. Occasionally you do need to know and then you need to use:

- int PyUnicode_KIND(PyObject *o)

which returns PyUnicode_1BYTE_KIND, PyUnicode_2BYTE_KIND or PyUnicode_4BYTE_KIND.

If you need a C type to store a code point then the API provides specific data types:

```
type Py_UCS4
type Py_UCS2
type Py_UCS1
```

Each is an unsigned integer which can store the indicated size of the code point. Notice that these are C types not Python types.

You can get the length of the string using;

- Py_ssize_t PyUnicode_GET_LENGTH(PyObject *o)

Notice that this isn't the number of bytes that the string uses, but the number of Unicode characters it contains.

Creating Unicode Strings

You can create an empty Unicode object using:

- `PyObject *PyUnicode_New(Py_ssize_t size, Py_UCS4 maxchar)`

The number of bytes used per code point is determined by `maxchar`. This is the largest code point you are going to use with the new string rounded up to one of 127, 255, 65535, 1114111 and selecting 1, 1, 2, 4 bytes per element respectively. The size parameter specifies the number of elements the new object has. In principle, a Python string is immutable, but to set values in the new Unicode string you have use:

- `Py_ssize_t PyUnicode_Fill(PyObject *unicode,`
  `     Py_ssize_t start,Py_ssize_t length, Py_UCS4 fill_char)`
- `int PyUnicode_WriteChar(PyObject *unicode,`
  `                      Py_ssize_t index, Py_UCS4 character)`

The `Fill` function will fill a slice of the new object with the code point given by `fill_char`. The `WriteChar` function stores the code point at the specified element. In both cases the code point specified has to be the right range to be stored in the element, i.e. one, two or four bytes.

For example:

```
static PyObject *string1(PyObject *self, PyObject *args)
{
    PyObject *uni1 = PyUnicode_New(10, 255);
    PyUnicode_Fill(uni1, 0, 10, 120);
    PyUnicode_WriteChar(uni1, 0, 72);
    return uni1;
}
```

The Unicode object only allocates a single byte per element and hence the `Fill` and `WriteChar` functions are restricted to using characters in the range 0 to 255. The three functions create a string:

Hxxxxxxxxx

There are also two functions that let you work with the buffer in the Unicode object directly:

- `void *PyUnicode_DATA(PyObject *o)`
- `void PyUnicode_WRITE(int kind, void *data, Py_ssize_t index,`
  `                                    Py_UCS4 value)`

The `DATA` function returns a void pointer to the Unicode buffer which you can use in the `WRITE` function as data. You have to specify the kind of the Unicode object and no checks are performed to make sure you have this correct. You can use the `KIND` function to check.

Of course, as Python strings are immutable you should only use `Fill` and `Write` on strings you have created within the C function and have not yet returned to Python. Do not modify Python strings.

135

There are a number of functions that allow you to build a Unicode string from a C object:

- `PyObject *PyUnicode_FromString(const char *u)`
- `PyObject *PyUnicode_FromStringAndSize(const char *u, Py_ssize_t size)`
- `PyObject *PyUnicode_FromKindAndData(int kind, const void *buffer, Py_ssize_t size)`

The C string has to be UTF-8 encoded and, unless you specify the size, contain no embedded NULLs. The Unicode string will use as many bytes per element as needed to represent the characters in the C string. The FromKindAndData converts a string with a specified size into a Unicode string with the specified number of bytes per element depending on its kind that is one of PyUnicode_1BYTE_KIND, PyUnicode_2BYTE_KIND or PyUnicode_4BYTE_KIND. Each function returns a new Unicode string object with its reference count set to one.

The most sophisticated way of converting C data to a Unicode string is:

- `PyObject *PyUnicode_FromFormat(const char *format, …)`

there is also:

- `PyObject *PyUnicode_Format(PyObject *format, PyObject *args)`

which does the same thing but using Python objects for the format and values – format is a Python string and args is a tuple of Python objects.

Again, this uses the same format specifiers as printf to convert a list of C variable into a Unicode string:

Format	Type
%%	Escape for %
%c	int
%d	int
%u	unsigned int
%ld	long
%li	long
%lu	unsigned long
%lld	long long
%lli	long long
%llu	unsigned long long
%zd	Py_ssize_t
%zi	Py_ssize_t
%zu	size_t
%i	int
%x	int
%s	const char*
%p	const void*

There are also some that are unique:

Format	Type	
%A	PyObject*	`ascii()`
%U	PyObject*	Unicode object
%V	PyObject*, const char*	Unicode object, C string alternative
%S	PyObject*	Result of calling `str()`
%R	PyObject*	Result of calling `repr()`

For example:

```
PyObject *uni1=PyUnicode_FromFormat("Hello World %d", 42);
```

creates a string containing:

```
Hello World 42
```

There are also some functions that allow you to transfer data from other Python objects:

- `PyObject *PyUnicode_FromObject(PyObject *obj)`
- `Py_ssize_t PyUnicode_CopyCharacters(PyObject *to,
                    Py_ssize_t to_start, PyObject *from,
                    Py_ssize_t from_start, Py_ssize_t how_many)`

The FromObject function can be used to convert a Unicode subtype to a true Unicode string. If the object is already a true Unicode string, no new object is created and the original string is returned with its reference count incremented. Unlike FromObject, the CopyCharacters function will, always return a new object by copying the code points from the from Unicode string to the to Unicode string. The start and how_many determine the substring of the from object that is copied. Unless a format conversion is required from one kind to another, such as from PyUnicode_1BYTE_KIND to PyUnicode_2BYTE_KIND, a fast memcpy is used.

Python strings can be cached in such a way that only one copy of the string is stored, no matter how many times you create a Unicode object with the same content. This is called "interning". This happens automatically for small strings, but if you want to be sure that you only create one string object with a given value then you can use:

- `void PyUnicode_InternInPlace(PyObject **str)`
- `PyObject *PyUnicode_InternFromString(const char *v)`

The first interns an existing Python string object and the second converts a C string into a Python string and interns it. If the Python string isn't in the collection it is simply added to the collection. If the Python string is already in the collection its reference count is decremented and str is set to reference it instead.

Characters

There are several predicates that can be used to test the type of a Unicode character:

- `int Py_UNICODE_ISSPACE(Py_UCS4 ch)`
- `int Py_UNICODE_ISLOWER(Py_UCS4 ch)`
- `int Py_UNICODE_ISUPPER(Py_UCS4 ch)`
- `int Py_UNICODE_ISTITLE(Py_UCS4 ch)`
- `int Py_UNICODE_ISLINEBREAK(Py_UCS4 ch)`
- `int Py_UNICODE_ISDECIMAL(Py_UCS4 ch)`
- `int Py_UNICODE_ISDIGIT(Py_UCS4 ch)`
- `int Py_UNICODE_ISNUMERIC(Py_UCS4 ch)`
- `int Py_UNICODE_ISALPHA(Py_UCS4 ch)`
- `int Py_UNICODE_ISALNUM(Py_UCS4 ch)`
- `int Py_UNICODE_ISPRINTABLE(Py_UCS4 ch)`

There are also functions which can convert a Unicode character to something else:

- `int Py_UNICODE_TODECIMAL(Py_UCS4 ch)`
- `int Py_UNICODE_TODIGIT(Py_UCS4 ch)`
- `double Py_UNICODE_TONUMERIC(Py_UCS4 ch)`

Manipulating Python Strings

The C API supports a reduced set of string manipulation functions:

- `Py_UCS4 PyUnicode_ReadChar(PyObject *unicode,`
`Py_ssize_t index)`
- `PyObject *PyUnicode_Substring(PyObject *str,`
`Py_ssize_t start,Py_ssize_t end)`
- `PyObject *PyUnicode_Concat(PyObject *strleft,`
`PyObject *strright)`
- `PyObject *PyUnicode_Split(PyObject *str, PyObject *strsep,`
`Py_ssize_t maxsplit)`
- `PyObject *PyUnicode_Splitlines(PyObject *str, int keepend)`
- `PyObject *PyUnicode_Join(PyObject *separator, PyObject *seq)`
- `PyObject *PyUnicode_Replace(PyObject *str, PyObject *substr,`
`PyObject *replstr, Py_ssize_t maxcount)`

These all return a new string with a reference count of one and mostly work like the equivalent Python string functions. Notice that the `ReadChar` function always returns a four-byte code point and not a string.

There are two functions that allow you to extract the full Unicode representation of the string in a C array:

- `Py_UCS4 *PyUnicode_AsUCS4(PyObject *str, Py_UCS4 *buffer,`
`Py_ssize_t buflen, int copy_null)`
- `Py_UCS4 *PyUnicode_AsUCS4Copy(PyObject *str)`

The first accepts a buffer filled with the code points that are stored in `str`. The second does the same job, but it creates a buffer using `PyMem_Malloc`.

Both return a pointer to the buffer. You have to ensure that the buffer is freed when you are finished with the data. It doesn't matter what kind of string str is, its elements are expanded to four bytes – padded with zeros as necessary. The copy_null parameter can be set to one to include a NULL at the end of the buffer. The Copy function always adds a NULL.

For example:

```
PyObject *myString = PyUnicode_FromString("Spam, Spam, Spam,
                            Spam... Lovely Spam! Wonderful Spam!");
int len = PyUnicode_GET_LENGTH(myString);
Py_UCS4 *buf = PyMem_Malloc(sizeof(Py_UCS4) * (len+1));
PyUnicode_AsUCS4(myString, buf, 100, 1);
for (int i = 0; buf[i]; i++)
{
  printf("%04X ", buf[i]);
}
PyMem_Free(buf);
```

Notice that the buffer has to be large enough to hold the string and the NULL and we need to remember to free the buffer.

Using the Copy function for the same task is easier, but we still have to remember to free the buffer:

```
buf = PyUnicode_AsUCS4Copy(myString);
for (int i = 0; buf[i]; i++)
{
  printf("%04X ", buf[i]);
}
PyMem_Free(buf);
```

We also need to remember to decrement the reference count of any Python strings that have been created and are no longer needed.

A complete function demonstrating both approaches is:

```
static PyObject *string2(PyObject *self, PyObject *args)
{
  PyObject *myString = PyUnicode_FromString("Spam, Spam, Spam,
                          Spam... Lovely Spam! Wonderful Spam!");
  int len = PyUnicode_GET_LENGTH(myString);
  Py_UCS4 *buf = PyMem_Malloc(sizeof(Py_UCS4) * (len + 1));
  PyUnicode_AsUCS4(myString, buf, 100, 1);
  for (int i = 0; buf[i]; i++)
  {
    printf("%04X ", buf[i]);
  }
  PyMem_Free(buf);
  printf("\n\n");
  buf = PyUnicode_AsUCS4Copy(myString);
```

```
for (int i = 0; buf[i]; i++)
{
  printf("%04X ", buf[i]);
}
printf("\n\n");
PyMem_Free(buf);
Py_DECREF(myString);
Py_RETURN_NONE;
}
```

Search

There are also text search functions. Find locates a substring in another string:

- Py_ssize_t PyUnicode_Find(PyObject *str, PyObject *substr,
              Py_ssize_t start, Py_ssize_t end, int direction)

For example:

```
PyObject *myString = PyUnicode_FromString("Spam, Spam, Spam, Spam…
                          Lovely Spam! Wonderful Spam!");
int len = PyUnicode_GET_LENGTH(myString);
PyObject *substr = PyUnicode_FromString("Lovely");

Py_ssize_t pos = PyUnicode_Find(myString, substr, 0, len, 1);
printf("position of Lovely = %ld\n", pos);
```

displays position of Lovely = 24.

FindChar works in the same way as Find but for a single character:

- Py_ssize_t PyUnicode_FindChar(PyObject *str, Py_UCS4 ch,
              Py_ssize_t start, Py_ssize_t end, int direction)

For example:

```
pos = PyUnicode_FindChar(myString, 0x0000006D, 0, len, 1);
printf("position of first m %ld\n", pos);
```

where 0x0000006D is Unicode for small m. This displays the position of the first m i.e. 3.

Tailmatch tests to see if the substring is a match at the start, direction=-1, or end, direction=1, of the slice of the string.

- Py_ssize_t PyUnicode_Tailmatch(PyObject *str,
                    PyObject *substr,Py_ssize_t start,
                        Py_ssize_t end, int direction)

For example:

```
substr = PyUnicode_FromString("Spam");
Py_ssize_t result = PyUnicode_Tailmatch(myString, substr,
                                        0,len, -1);
printf("prefix match %ld\n", result);
```

displays prefix match 1.

The Contains function returns true if the substring is contained in the string:

- ◆ int PyUnicode_Contains(PyObject *str, PyObject *substr)

For example:

```
result =PyUnicode_Contains(myString,substr);
printf("Contains Spam %ld\n", result);
```

displays Contains Spam 1 because there is definitely Spam in it.

The Count function counts the number of times the substring is in the string:

```
Py_ssize_t PyUnicode_Count(PyObject *str, PyObject *substr,
                           Py_ssize_t start, Py_ssize_t end)
```

For example:

```
Py_ssize_t count = PyUnicode_Count(myString, substr, 0, len);
printf("Count of how many spam(s) %ld\n", count);
```

displays Count of how many spam(s) 6.

Finally there are three string compare functions:

- ◆ int PyUnicode_Compare(PyObject *left, PyObject *right)
- ◆ int PyUnicode_CompareWithASCIIString(PyObject *uni,
                                        const char *string)
- ◆ PyObject *PyUnicode_RichCompare(PyObject *left,
                                    PyObject *right, int op)

These are all fairly self explanatory. The Tailmatch function tests to see if the substring is at the start, direction=-1 or end, direction=1 of the string. The RichCompare can be used with a range of relational operators: Py_GT, Py_GE, Py_EQ, Py_NE, Py_LT, and Py_LE.

For example:

```
  PyObject *test = PyUnicode_FromString("Spam");
  result = PyUnicode_Compare(substr, test);
  printf("compare to Spam %ld\n", result);
  result = PyUnicode_CompareWithASCIIString(substr, "Spam");
  printf("compare to Spam %ld\n", result);
  PyObject *logic = PyUnicode_RichCompare(substr, test, Py_EQ);
  if (Py_IsTrue(logic))
  {
    printf("Strings are equal");
  }
  else
  {
    printf("Strings are not equal");
  }
```

All three test for equality between "Spam" and "Spam" The only complication is the way that RichCompare returns a Python True or False objects and this has to be tested for using IsTrue to be useful in C.

Notice that all of the Python strings created in these examples have to have their reference counts decremented to zero so that they are garbage-collected unless they are used further by the Python program or another C function.

You can see a listing of the string3 function, which puts all of these examples together, on the book's webpage.

Encoding

Python may use Unicode internally, but the outside world uses various encodings of Unicode, many of which only manage to represent a small subset of the full range of code points. The problems of converting a string from Unicode to another representation, i.e. encoding, and converting a representation to Unicode, i.e. decoding, are very common. Fortunately Python, and hence the Python C API, make it very easy by providing a range of codecs (COderDECoder) that are written in C and perform the job very efficiently.

There is a pair of general functions that will use any available codec by name:

- ```
  PyObject *PyUnicode_Decode(const char *s, Py_ssize_t size,
                          const char *encoding, const char *errors)
  ```
- ```
  PyObject *PyUnicode_AsEncodedString(PyObject *unicode,
                          const char *encoding, const char *errors)
  ```

The first takes a C string coded using the encoding specified and converts it into a Python Unicode string. The second does the reverse process, but instead of returning a C string it returns a bytes object. As it is very possible that characters cannot always be converted, errors controls how encoding/decoding errors are handled. If errors is set to 'strict' (the default), a UnicodeError exception is raised. Other possible values are 'ignore', 'replace', 'xmlcharrefreplace', 'backslashreplace' and any other name registered via codecs.register_error() in the Python program you are working with.

There is also:

- ```
  PyObject *PyUnicode_FromEncodedObject(PyObject *obj,
                         const char *encoding, const char *errors)
  ```

which will create a Python Unicode string from any bytes-like object using the specified decoder.

A very large number of codecs are supported and you can look them up in the documentation, but there are a few important ones that are worth explaining.
  ```

UTF and UCS

There is a lot of confusion about the differences between UTF Unicode Transformation format and UCS Universal Character Set. UTF-n is an encoding using n-bit words that can encode the entire 21-bit Unicode range, using a variable number of words if necessary. UCSn uses n bytes to represent the sub-range of Unicode characters that are within its range. For example, UTF-8 uses 1, 2, 3 or 4 bytes to represent the entire Unicode range whereas UCS1 uses a single byte to represent just the extended ASCII characters, i.e. code points 0 to 255.

Python, and the Python C API in particular, uses UCS in a way that isn't particularly standard, though it is logical. Originally UCS2, i.e. 16-bit Unicode was the entire Unicode range until the range was extended to 21 bits. As a result UCS2 couldn't access the full range and UTF-16 was introduced to solve the problem. UTF-16 is a variable length encoding and allows some code points to be represented by two 16-bit values. To make this possible, a block of code points was set aside and not allocated printable characters – the surrogate range 0xDC00 to 0xDFF. This is split into two sub-blocks: the high surrogate range is 0xD800 to 0xDBFF and the low surrogate range 0xDC00 to 0xDFFF. These values have no printable forms and are present to allow other Unicode characters to be represented as two 16-bit values. That is, a single code point in either surrogate range has no assigned meaning. When a high surrogate, H, is immediately followed by a low surrogate, L, the pair encodes a code point given by:

```
0x10000 + (H - 0xD800) × 0x400 + (L - 0xDC00)
```

The surrogate representation is used in UTF-16 encoding to allow the full range of Unicode to be represented either by a single 16-bit word or two 16-bit words in the surrogate range.

There are some function to help with working with surrogates:

- `int Py_UNICODE_IS_SURROGATE(ch)`
- `int Py_UNICODE_IS_HIGH_SURROGATE(ch)`
- `int Py_UNICODE_IS_LOW_SURROGATE(ch)`
- `Py_UCS4 Py_UNICODE_JOIN_SURROGATES(high, low)`

The `JOIN_SURROGATES` function can be used to combine two 16-bit surrogates to create a single 2- bit code point stored in four bytes as a UCS4.

Although these functions allow you to convert surrogates manually, it is more usual to allow the UTF-16 codec do the job automatically.

Notice that the 16-bit word of UCS2 should not contain a surrogate code point as they are never interpreted in pairs.

Similarly, UCS1 is a single-byte representation of code points in the range 0 to 255 and UTF-8 is a variable-byte representation of the complete range of code points. UTF-8 can use as many as four bytes to store a code point using the scheme outlined in the table:

First code point	Last code point	Byte 1	Byte 2	Byte 3	Byte 4
U+0000	U+007F	0xxxxxxx			
U+0080	U+07FF	110xxxxx	10xxxxxx		
U+0800	U+FFFF	1110xxxx	10xxxxxx	10xxxxxx	
U+10000	U+10FFFF	11110xxx	10xxxxxx	10xxxxxx	10xxxxxx

As you can see, up to code point 127 UTF-8 agrees with UCS1. Notice that UTF-8 doesn't make use of surrogate pairs or any modification of Unicode.

Of course, there is also UTF-32 which is identical to UCS4 and involves no encoding at all as the full range of code points can be stored without modification.

There is a decode function for each UTF encoding:

- ◆ PyObject *PyUnicode_DecodeUTF8(const char *s,
                              Py_ssize_t size,constchar*errors)
- ◆ PyObject *PyUnicode_DecodeUTF16(const char *s,
             Py_ssize_t size, const char *errors, int *byteorder)
- ◆ PyObject *PyUnicode_DecodeUTF32(const char *s,
             Py_ssize_t size,const char *errors, int *byteorder)

Each takes an encoded C string and converts it to a Python Unicode string. The UTF16 and UTF32 decoders have the additional problem of coping with byte order:

```
*byteorder == -1:   little endian
*byteorder ==  0:   native order
*byteorder ==  1:   big endian
```

Native order is optionally determined by the first two/four bytes from a Byte Order Mark, BOM. The BOM is code point FEFF and reading FE followed by FF suggests that the order is big endian. In UTF-32 the BOM is followed by two NULL bytes. After decoding is complete byteorder is set to the byte order actually used.

There are also Stateful version of the decoders which will decode until they reach invalid characters and return the number of characters decoded.

The encode functions are very simple:

- ◆ PyObject *PyUnicode_AsUTF8String(PyObject *unicode)
- ◆ PyObject *PyUnicode_AsUTF16String(PyObject *unicode)
- ◆ PyObject *PyUnicode_AsUTF32String(PyObject *unicode)

Each one takes a Python Unicode string and returns a Python bytes object using the specified encoding.

As UTF-8 is so commonly used there are two additional encoders for it:

- ◆ const char *PyUnicode_AsUTF8(PyObject *unicode)
- ◆ const char *PyUnicode_AsUTF8AndSize(PyObject *unicode,
                                      Py_ssize_t *size)

These return a NULL terminated C string.

For example, to encode to each of the UTF formats:

```
static PyObject *string4(PyObject *self, PyObject *args)
{
  PyObject *myString = PyUnicode_FromString("Spam, Spam, Spam, Spam
                        . . .Lovely Spam! Wonderful Spam!");
  PyObject *bytesUTF8 = PyUnicode_AsUTF8String(myString);
  PyObject *bytesUTF16 = PyUnicode_AsUTF16String(myString);
  PyObject *bytesUTF32 = PyUnicode_AsUTF32String(myString);
  Py_ssize_t len = PyBytes_Size(bytesUTF32);
  for (int i = 0; i < len; i++)
  {
    PyObject *item = PySequence_GetItem(bytesUTF32, i);
    int c = PyLong_AsLong(item);
    printf("%02X ", c);
  }
```

This example prints the bytes that correspond to UTF-32 which starts:

```
FF  FE  00  00  53  00  00  00  70  00  00  00
and so on...
```

The first two characters are the BOM indicating little endian encoding.

To demonstrate that the encoding is correct we can complete the "round trip" by converting the bytes object to a UTF-32 C string and converting this back to a Python Unicode string:

```
  char *buffer;
  PyBytes_AsStringAndSize(bytesUTF32, &buffer, &len);
  PyObject *decodeStr = PyUnicode_DecodeUTF32(buffer, len,
                                           NULL, NULL);

  return decodeStr;
}
```

Notice that as the bytes object contains embedded NULLs we need to use the len variable to determine its length. You can try the other encoding in the same way. Notice that decrementing the reference counts of the many objects created has been omitted.

Wide Character Support

C introduced the wchar_t type as a way of representing the complete Unicode range of code points. Initially wchar_t was set at 16 bits, which was enough to do the job and was equivalent to UCS2. Just as UCS2 was made obsolete by the extension of Unicode to 21-bits, so was wchar_t implemented at 16-bits. Some platforms redefine it as 32-bits and in this form it is equivalent to UCS4 and hence full Unicode. However, most platforms, Windows in particular, have stuck with wchar_t as 16 bits.

The C API provides a single function which will create a Python Unicode string from a wchar_t array:

- PyObject *PyUnicode_FromWideChar(const wchar_t *w,
                                                           Py_ssize_t size)

If you pass size=-1 the function works out the size of the NULL-terminated wchar_t string. If wchar_t is 16-bit this function will detect and convert surrogate pairs and hence it treats the wchar_t string as being UTF-16 encoded.

There are two functions which encode a Python Unicode string as a wchar_t array:

- Py_ssize_t PyUnicode_AsWideChar(PyObject *unicode,
                                                          wchar_t *w, Py_ssize_t
  size)
- wchar_t *PyUnicode_AsWideCharString(PyObject *unicode,
                                                              Py_ssize_t *size)

The difference between them is that the first needs a wchar_t buffer passed in and the second creates the buffer for you. Of course, you have to use PyMem_Free() to free the generated buffer. If you set size to NULL a full NULL terminated string is returned with no embedded NULLs. If wchar_t is 16-bit and the Unicode character cannot be represented in 16-bits then a surrogate pair is generated, i.e. the resulting wchar_t string is encoded as UTF-16. If wchar_t is 32-bit then these functions reduce to a copy operation.

Code Pages

Before Unicode systems displayed characters beyond the basic ASCII using "code pages". A code page provides a range of 256 characters that can be displayed. Characters were selected using extended ASCII, i.e. the first 128 characters are standard ASCII and the custom characters correspond to codes above 127. So to display a character that is not part of the ASCII character set you first select a code page that has it and then use its code in the code page. Of course, if the machine has a different code page selected then the code you use will not correspond to the character you want. Each code above 127 corresponds to a range of different characters depending on the code page that is active.

You can make use of code pages on Windows machines using the Code Page's codec. For example:

```
PyObject *myBytes = PyUnicode_AsEncodedString(myString,
                                             "cp1252", NULL);
```

encodes the string according to cp1252, Code Page 1252, i.e. the Latin Code page for Windows and stores a pointer to the result as a bytes object in myBytes.

A function to encode a string into the Latin code page is:

```
static PyObject *string5(PyObject *self, PyObject *args)
{
    PyObject *myString = PyUnicode_New(1, 1114111);
    PyUnicode_WriteChar(myString, 0, 0x2020);
    PyObject *myBytes = PyUnicode_AsEncodedString(
                            myString, "cp1252", NULL);
    char *buffer;
    Py_ssize_t len;
    PyBytes_AsStringAndSize(myBytes, &buffer, &len);
    printf("%X \n", buffer[0]);
    printf("%s \n", buffer);
    Py_DECREF(myBytes);
    return myString;
}
```

Unicode character 0x2020 is † i.e. a dagger symbol and this doesn't occur in the ASCII code but it is character 0x86 in the Latin code page. If you run the program above under Windows you will probably see:

```
86
å
```

The 86 corresponds to the code for the dagger in the Latin code page which is what was requested. The character you see printed depends on what code page the editor's terminal is using. In the example above it is the Windows terminal which uses code page 850 Latin-1 by default and code 0x86 is "Lower case a with ring above". You can see that the Unicode dagger has been converted to the correct code page code, but what you actually see depends on what code page or Unicode the terminal is set to.

Locale and File System Encoding

The setting of the locale can be used to decode/encode strings obtained from the operating system into Unicode. There are two decoders:

- ```
  PyObject *PyUnicode_DecodeLocale(const char *str,
                                   const char *errors)
  ```
- ```
  PyObject *PyUnicode_DecodeLocaleAndSize(const char *str,
            Py_ssize_t len, const char *errors)
  ```

The first will decode the C string to Unicode using the appropriate codec for the locale. The second does the same thing, but specifies the length of the string.

The encoding function returns a byte object encoded as suitable for the current local:

- ```
  PyObject *PyUnicode_EncodeLocale(PyObject *unicode,
                                   const char *errors)
  ```

The operating system will use a particular encoding for its environment strings and for file system names. There are two decode functions and one encode function:

- ```
  PyObject *PyUnicode_DecodeFSDefault(const char *s)
  ```
- ```
  PyObject *PyUnicode_DecodeFSDefaultAndSize(const char *s,
                                             Py_ssize_t size)
  ```
- ```
  PyObject *PyUnicode_EncodeFSDefault(PyObject *unicode)
  ```

These both convert between Python Unicode strings and C strings.

There are two conversion functions specifically for use with file paths:

- ```
  int PyUnicode_FSConverter(PyObject *obj, void *result)
  ```
- ```
  int PyUnicode_FSDecoder(PyObject *obj, void *result)
  ```

The obj should be a Python string or a Pathlike object representing a path. The result is a bytes-like object.

Codecs

The Python system of codecs is extensive and it is easy to add to the library if you need to implement a custom codec. There are also many codecs that don't fit into the simple idea of a codec. Some are more like general text processors. For example:

```
static PyObject *string6(PyObject *self, PyObject *args)
{
  PyObject *myString = PyUnicode_FromString("† Spam, Spam, Spam,
                         Spam . . .Lovely Spam! Wonderful Spam!");
  PyObject *myBytes = PyUnicode_AsEncodedString(myString,
                              "raw_unicode_escape", NULL);
  Py_DECREF(myString);
  return myBytes;
}
```

This converts a Unicode string into an escaped Latin 1 extended ASCII encoding that includes \uXXXX and \UXXXXXXXX escape codes for code points that cannot be represented. In the example there is a "dagger" symbol, u2020, and the output is:

```
 b'\\u2020 Spam, Spam, Spam, Spam . . .Lovely Spam!
                                        Wonderful Spam!'
```

Not all of the listed codecs can be used in this way – some only accept bytes objects as input for encoding and decoding and these are slightly more difficult to use and need to be called using;

```
PyObject *PyCodec_Encode(PyObject *object, const char *encoding,
                                          const char *errors)

PyObject *PyCodec_Decode(PyObject *object, const char *encoding,
                                          const char *errors)
```

Summary

- Bytes and bytearray objects are immutable and mutable objects respectively that play the role that ASCII strings play in other languages.

- The byte and bytearray types are very useful in getting raw data to and from C functions

- A Python string is always Unicode, but how many bytes are used per element varies according to the largest code point being stored.

- There are C API function equivalents of most of the Python string functions.

- A key idea in working with Unicode strings is encoding and decoding.

- Python supports a range of codecs that can convert a Unicode string into an equivalent in a different encoding and vice versa.

- The most common encodings are UTF-8, UTF-16 and UTF-32. The easiest to use with C is UTF-8 because this can often be treated as ASCII.

- C doesn't have native support for Unicode or any of the standard encodings. It does support a wide 16-bit character type, but this is not standard and is not simple to work with.

- One of the most common use of encoding is to convert Unicode into the equivalent character in one of the many code pages that were used to extend the ASCII character set.

- If you can avoid using code pages then do so as it is not an easy thing to get right and very prone to being displayed in the wrong code page.

Chapter 11

Modules And Attributes

So far we have been using objects that have been created within Python programs or standard objects which API functions have been available to create. Python's principle of "everything is an object", the concept central to my book *Programmer's Python: Everything is an Object*, ISBN: 978-1871962741, applies just as much to the C API and this is the reason that the PyObject type is used everywhere. Of course, in a C program we have the added problem of converting back and forth from C types, but this isn't too difficult given the supplied API functions. Things start to get more interesting when we create new Python object types within the C program. What is interesting is that this gives us an opportunity to see more of the inner workings of Python.

Before we move on to look at how to create custom objects, it is worth finding out how to add and work with custom attributes and the object to add them to is the module. The reason is that a module is very much like a custom class in that we add functions and data to it in roughly the same way.

Working With Modules

Creating a Python module is the aim of the C extension API. A module can the thought of as a big class or type which has attributes that are other Python objects. For example, if myModule has a class called myClass then:

```
myModule.myClass
```

is a reference to it which can be used to modify it as if it was a simple attribute or call it as if it was a method. A C extension shared library has to create a Python module complete with all of the attributes needed to make use of it in a Python program. When a Python program uses:

```
import myModule
```

the only thing that happens is that Python calls the single exported function:

```
PyMODINIT_FUNC PyInit_myModule(void)
```

which has to return a Python module object complete with attributes ready to be used. That is, all of the other code in the shared library is executed as part of the Python program making use of the module – only the PyMODINIT_FUNC function is called by the system. This is single-phase initialization and it is good for most C extensions.

In this case the module behaves like a `class` that you cannot instantiate, i.e. a singleton, in the sense that if you load the module again you still have the same "instance" of the module. A multi-phase initialization is more like a regular Python module in that you get a new instance each time you load it and the old one is garbage-collected. Instances of the module should be independent so as to support sub-interpreters.

Adding Module Attributes

In most cases you can use a `PyModuleDef` struct with an array of `PyMethodDef` structs to define a set of module-level functions which are like module methods in the sense that when they are called `self` is set to reference the module. However, you aren't restricted to adding module attributes that are functions or even by using the `PyModuleDef` struct. You can add module attributes directly using;

- `int PyModule_AddObjectRef(PyObject *module, const char *name, PyObject *value)`
- `int PyModule_AddObject(PyObject *module, const char *name, PyObject *value)`

Both functions add an object given by `value` as an attribute of the module with the specified `name`. The difference between the two is that, on success, `ObjectRef` steals a reference to `value`, i.e. its reference count isn't changed, and this is usually what you want to do.

You can create a new module object with no additional attributes using:

```
static struct PyModuleDef myModule = {
    PyModuleDef_HEAD_INIT,
    "example",
    "C library to test API",
    -1,
    NULL};

PyMODINIT_FUNC PyInit_example(void)
{
    PyObject *m = PyModule_Create(&myModule);
```

The module is defined using a `PyModuleDef` struct without any methods defined, i.e. the final field is `NULL`.

Now that you have a module object you can add some attributes. For example:

```
PyObject *myValue = PyLong_FromLong(42);
PyModule_AddObject(m, "myValue", myValue);
```

After this the module has an integer attribute called `myValue`. Notice that the reference count for `myValue` is set to one which is correct. If the operation fails then you would probably need to decrement the reference count as `myValue` would not be required. The new attribute behaves as if it was a module variable:

```
import example
print("module constant",example.myValue)
example.myValue=43
print("module constant",example.myValue)
```

The first `print` displays 42 and the second 43.

You can add any Python object as an attribute. For example, to add a list:

```
PyObject *myList=PyList_New(0);
PyModule_AddObject(m, "myList", myList);
```

and you can use it from Python in the usual way:

```
print(example.myList)
example.myList.append("spam")
print(example.myList)
```

which displays [ ] followed by [*"spam"*].

The need to create module-level constants is so common there are some functions to do it:

- ◆ `int PyModule_AddIntConstant(PyObject *module,`
  `const char *name, long value)`
- ◆ `int PyModule_AddStringConstant(PyObject *module,`
  `const char *name,const char *value)`
- ◆ `int PyModule_AddIntMacro(PyObject *module, macro)`
- ◆ `int PyModule_AddStringMacro(PyObject *module, macro)`

So for example, adding the integer attribute could be written:

```
PyModule_AddIntConstant(m,"myValue",42);
```

The reference count for the value is set to one.

Adding Function Attributes

We already have a good and very easy way to add functions to a module using the `PyMethodDef` struct, but there are many reasons for wanting to add functions directly. For one thing the direct method works when adding functions to any object, not just a module.

There are two sorts of function that you can have in an extension module – Python functions and C functions. If you want to expose a C function as if it was a Python function then it has to be converted into a Python object. The simplest way of doing this is to use:

- ◆ `PyObject *PyCFunction_New(PyMethodDef *ml, PyObject *self)`
- ◆ `PyObject *PyCFunction_NewEx(PyMethodDef *ml,`
  `                        PyObject *self, PyObject *module)`
- ◆ `PyObject *PyCMethod_New(PyMethodDef *ml, PyObject *self,`
  `                       PyObject *module, PyTypeObject *cls)`

These three functions are currently undocumented, but this seems to be an oversight. They all take a `PyMethodDef` struct which defines the characteristics of the function as a Python function. The first simply creates the `PyCFunction` object and passes the `self` parameter when the function is called. For a module level function `self` should be the module object. The second and third functions set the function objects `__module__` attribute. The third function also records the `cls` and passes it on to the function when it is called in Python.

Currently the API supports five different ways to call a C function and these are set in the `PyMethodDef` stuct in the `ml_flags`:

- ◆ `METH_VARARGS`
  `PyObject *PyCFunction(PyObject *self,`
  `                        PyObject *args);`
- ◆ `METH_KEYWORDS`
  `PyObject *PyCFunctionWithKeywords(PyObject *self,`
  `                                    PyObject *args,`
  `                                    PyObject *kwargs);`
- ◆ `METH_FASTCALL`
  `PyObject *_PyCFunctionFast(PyObject *self,`
  `                             PyObject *const *args,`
  `                             Py_ssize_t nargs);`
- ◆ `METH_FASTCALL | METH_KEYWORDS`
  `PyObject *_PyCFunctionFastWithKeywords(PyObject *self,`
  `                                         PyObject *const *args,`
  `                                         Py_ssize_t nargs,`
  `                                         PyObject *kwnames);`
- ◆ `METH_METHOD | METH_FASTCALL | METH_KEYWORDS`
  `PyObject *PyCMethod(PyObject *self,`
  `                      PyTypeObject *defining_class,`
  `                      PyObject *const *args,`
  `                      Py_ssize_t nargs,`
  `                      PyObject *kwnames)`

The METH_VARARGS and METH_KEYWORDS pass the parameters as a tuple and dictionary of key words. The FASTCALL passes all parameters as an array and, if there are keyword parameters, kwnames is a tuple of keyword strings that can be used to identify the keyword parameters. The nargs parameter always gives the number of positional parameters and any keyword parameters come after the positional parameters. Finally the METH_METHOD adds a parameter, defining_class, for the class. Clearly you have to use PyCMethod to set the value of cls, and hence defining_class, when the function is called. Notice you can only use the flags in the given combinations.

This all seems complicated, but in practice it is surprisingly easy. For example, to add a simple C function that has only positional arguments you could use:

```
static PyObject *myFunc(PyObject *self, PyObject *args)
{
  printf("hello world\n");
  Py_RETURN_NONE;
}

static PyMethodDef myFunc_def = {
    "myFunc",
    myFunc,
    METH_VARARGS,
    "the doc string"};

static struct PyModuleDef myModule = {
    PyModuleDef_HEAD_INIT,
    "example",
    "C library to test API",
    -1,
    NULL};

PyMODINIT_FUNC PyInit_example(void)
{
  PyObject *m = PyModule_Create(&myModule);
  if (m == NULL)
    return NULL;
  PyObject *myPyFun = PyCFunction_New(&myFunc_def, m);
  PyModule_AddObject(m, "myFunc1", myPyFun);
  return m;
}
```

This sets the function's reference count to one. After this the function can be called from Python:

```
print(example.myFunc1())
```

Of course, you can process any parameters passed to the function using the techniques introduced in Chapter 5.

As another example we can add a FastCall function with keywords:

```c
static PyObject *myFunc2(PyObject *self, PyObject *const *args,
                              Py_ssize_t nargs, PyObject *kwnames)
{
  for (int i = 0; i < nargs; i++)
  {
    const char *myString = PyUnicode_AsUTF8(args[i]);
    printf("%s\n", myString);
  }
  Py_ssize_t nKwds = PyTuple_Size(kwnames);
  for (int i = 0; i < nKwds; i++)
  {
    const char *myValue = PyUnicode_AsUTF8(args[i + nargs]);
    const char *myKeyword =
                  PyUnicode_AsUTF8(PyTuple_GetItem(kwnames, i));
    printf("Keyword = %s, Value = %s \n", myKeyword, myValue);
  }
  Py_RETURN_NONE;
}

static PyMethodDef myFunc2_def = {
    "myFunc2",
    (PyCFunction)myFunc2,
    METH_FASTCALL | METH_KEYWORDS,
    "the doc string"};

PyMODINIT_FUNC PyInit_example(void)
{
  PyObject *m = PyModule_Create(&myModule);
  if (m == NULL)
    return NULL;

  PyObject *myPyFun2 = PyCFunction_New(&myFunc2_def, m);
  PyModule_AddObject(m, "myFunc2", myPyFun2);

  return m;
}
```

This will print the positional parameters followed by the keyword parameters. The first for loop processes the positional parameters in the first nargs elements and the second loop processes the keyword parameters in the remaining nKwds elements. If you try it out with something like:

```python
example.myFunc2("Hello","World",MyKeyWord="myValue")
```

it displays:

```
Hello
World
Keyword = MyKeyWord, Value = myValue
```

A real example would need to check the types of the parameters and the keywords used.

156

Functions In Other Modules

You can add functions, Python or C, defined in other modules as attributes of the extension module you are creating. After all, once converted to a `PyObject`, a C function looks just like a Python function from the point of view of its caller.

The first problem we have to solve is finding the module that the function is in. For example, if you want to add the `math.sqrt` function as an attribute of your module you would first need a reference to the `math` module.

Assuming that this is loaded you can use the:

- `PyObject *PyImport_AddModuleObject(PyObject *name)`
- `PyObject *PyImport_AddModule(const char *name)`

functions. They differ only in how the module is specified – by a Python string or a C string. This returns a reference to the specified module without incrementing its reference count. Notice that the module has to already loaded otherwise it returns a `NULL`.

Once you have a reference to the module you can use:

- `PyObject *PyModule_GetDict(PyObject *module)`

to get the module's dict and this in turn can be used to get any attribute of the module via:

- `PyObject *PyDict_GetItemString(PyObject *p, const char *key)`

Putting all this together we can easily add the `sqrt` function to the module:

```
PyObject *math = PyImport_AddModule("math");
PyObject *mathdict = PyModule_GetDict(math);
PyObject *myFunction = PyDict_GetItemString(mathdict, "sqrt");
PyModule_AddObject(m, "myFunc3", myFunction);
```

If the module isn't loaded then this won't work. If you want the extension module to load the module you can replace `AddModule` by

```
PyObject *math=PyImport_ImportModule("math");
```

You can now try it out using:

```
print(example.myFunc3(2))
print(example.myFunc3.__name__)
```

which displays

```
1.4142135623730951
sqrt
```

If you want to use a function defined in the main module simply use the module name `__main__`.

Multi-phase initialization

So far we have been using single phase initialization of modules which is sufficient for most extension modules but its not the best way to do the job. The problem is that C modules don't behave like Python modules. A Python module is first created and then its code is executed. This parallels the usual new and init stages in the construction of a class.

Although we have been using single-phase initialization in all the examples so far, it is important to understand that multi-phase is the modern way to do the job. In particular, if you want you module to benefit from many of the improvements in the way modules are handled or to be speeded up by the implementation of sub-interpreters, then you should use multi-phase initialization. Notice that this only makes a difference when your extension module is used in a multi-threaded Python program, but this is becoming increasingly the case, see Chapter 14.

To make an extension module behave more like a Python module you need to use multi-phase initialization, which in theory uses any number of functions to create and initialize the module but in practice usually has only two - create and init.

To request multi-phase the PyMODINIT_FUNC has to return, not a module object, but a PyModuleDef struct with a non-empty m_slots field and initialized using:

   ◆   PyObject *PyModuleDef_Init(PyModuleDef *def)

How this works depends on the setting of m_slots in the module definition. This consists of an array of structs of the form:

```
type PyModuleDef_Slot{
int slot;
void *value:
}
```

What *value* means depends on the slot and at the moment there are only two possibilities:

Py_mod_create

means that value is a pointer to a create function with signature:

```
PyObject *create_module(PyObject *spec, PyModuleDef *def)
```

which creates the module using the spec and def given. There should only be one mod_create slot in the array. The spec is a ModuleSpec which contains additional information about the module which isn't set in a single-phase initialization.

You can see the correspondence between the attributes set on `ModuleSpec` and how they affect the module in the table below:

ModuleSpec attribute	Module attribute
name	__name__
loader	__loader__
parent	__package__
origin	__file__
cached	__cached__
submodule_search_locations	__path__
loader_state	
has_location	

If you don't specify a `mod_create` slot then a module is created for you.

The only other slot value is:

`Py_mod_exec`

means that the value is a pointer to an initialization function which plays the role of executing the module's code, i.e. it creates the module's attributes. The exec function has the signature:

`int exec_module(PyObject *module)`

As an example of using two-phase initialization, the following program creates a module using the `create` function and then initializes it using exec. For simplicity, the `create` function uses `PyModule_New`, but it also prints the value of one of attributes of `spec` to show how it is done. The `exec` function simply adds an integer attribute:

```
#define PY_SSIZE_T_CLEAN
#include <Python.h>

int exec(PyObject *m)
{
  PyObject *myValue = PyLong_FromLong(42);
  PyModule_AddObject(m, "myValue", myValue);
  return 0;
}
```

```
PyObject *create(PyObject *spec, PyModuleDef *def)
{
  PyObject *res=PyObject_GetAttrString(spec,"origin");
  printf("%s\n",PyUnicode_AsUTF8(res));
  PyObject *m= PyModule_New("example");

  return m;
}

PyModuleDef_Slot twoPhase[] = {
    {Py_mod_create, create},
    {Py_mod_exec, exec},
    {0, 0}};

static struct PyModuleDef myModuledef = {
    PyModuleDef_HEAD_INIT,
    "example",
    "C library to test API",
    0,
    NULL,
    twoPhase};

PyMODINIT_FUNC PyInit_example(void)
{
  return PyModuleDef_Init(&myModuledef);
}
```

Notice the way that the m_size field is now set to 0 rather than -1. In the next section we discover how this field is used in a more general setting.

In practice, you can use the create function to customize the module in more complicated ways, but for most extensions this is unnecessary and you can even remove the {Py_mod_create, create} from the array and let the system create the module for you.

Module Storage

To ensure isolation between instances of the module, which is needed when working with sub-interpreters, you can set up a per-module storage system. The m_size field in the PyModuleDef stuct can be set to the amount of storage that needs to be set aside for the module. Any of the module's attributes can access the module's state using:

```
void *PyModule_GetState(PyObject *module)
```

which returns a void pointer to the block of memory. To be clear, you should use this module local storage in place of global statics.

For example, if you want to store something that is accessible to all of the module's functions you might have used:

```
struct myData
{
  int count;
  char name[20];
};

static struct myData myModuleData = {42, "spam"};
```

The static struct can now be used within any of the module's functions. For example:

```
static PyObject *myFunc(PyObject *self, PyObject *args)
{
  printf("module data %d , %s\n", myModuleData.count,
                                        myModuleData.name);
  myModuleData.count++;
  Py_RETURN_NONE;
}
```

The problem is that myModuleData is shared between all of the instances of the module.

The correct way to implement static global data is to use module-local storage. The first thing we have to do is set the size of the memory to be allocated in the PyModuleDef struct:

```
static struct PyModuleDef myModuledef = {
    PyModuleDef_HEAD_INIT,
    "example",
    "C library to test API",
    sizeof(struct myData),
    NULL,
    twoPhase};
```

Now we have to arrange to initialize the storage. As this is only created after the create function has finished, we need to do this in the exec function:

```
int exec(PyObject *m)
{
  struct myData *myModData = (struct myData *)PyModule_GetState(m);
  myModData->count = 42;
  strcpy(myModData->name, "spam");

  PyObject *myPyFun = PyCFunction_New(&myFunc_def, m);
  PyModule_AddObject(m, "myFunc", myPyFun);

  return 0;
}
```

Notice that we also add a function attribute, myFunc1. This can also use the module-local storage:

```
static PyObject *myFunc(PyObject *self, PyObject *args)
{
  printf("module data %d, %s\n", myModuleData.count,
                                  myModuleData.name);
  myModuleData.count++;
  struct myData *myModData =
                  (struct myData *)PyModule_GetState(self);
  printf("module data %d, %s\n", myModData->count,
                                 myModData->name);
  myModData->count++;
  Py_RETURN_NONE;
}
```

The first part of the function uses the static global struct and the second part does the same thing using the module-local storage, in practice you should only use the module-local storage. If you try this out:

```
import example
example.myFunc()
example.myFunc()
```

you will see:

```
module data 42, spam
module data 42, spam
module data 43, spam
module data 43, spam
```

Finally this raises the question of cleaning up when the module is deallocated. There are three fields in the PyModuleDef struct that specify functions involved in garbage-collection:

- traverseproc m_traverse

  is called when the garbage collector is traversing the module, see Chapter 14.

- inquiry m_clear

  is called when the garbage collector is clearing the module and

- freefunc m_free

  which is called when the garbage collector is about to remove the module.

The first two are used to control the operation of the garbage collector and can usually be set to NULL but the m_free field has to be set to a function that will deallocate any memory that has been allocated on the heap.

For example:

```
void freeModule(void *m){
    struct myData *myModData =
                        (struct myData *)PyModule_GetState(m);
    PyMem_Free(myModData);
}

static struct PyModuleDef myModuledef = {
    PyModuleDef_HEAD_INIT,
    "example",
    "C library to test API",
    sizeof(struct myData),
    NULL,
    twoPhase,
    NULL,
    NULL,
    freeModule};
```

Notice that any memory you have allocated has to be freed using free() and any memory that Python has allocated has to be freed using PyMem_Free.

Of course, if you haven't allocated any memory and haven't asked for any module state memory, you can ignore m_free.

The complete program is:

```
#define PY_SSIZE_T_CLEAN
#include <Python.h>

struct myData
{
  int count;
  char name[20];
};

static struct myData myModuleData = {42, "spam"};

static PyObject *myFunc(PyObject *self, PyObject *args)
{
  printf("module data %d , %s\n",
                    myModuleData.count, myModuleData.name);
  myModuleData.count++;

  struct myData *myModData = (struct myData *)
                                    PyModule_GetState(self);
  printf("module data %d , %s\n", myModData→count,
                                    myModData->name);
  myModData->count++;

  Py_RETURN_NONE;
}
```

```
static PyMethodDef myFunc_def = {
    "myFunc",
    myFunc,
    METH_VARARGS,
    "the doc string"};

int exec(PyObject *m)
{
  struct myData *myModData = (struct myData *)PyModule_GetState(m);
  myModData->count = 42;
  strcpy(myModData->name, "spam");
  PyObject *myValue = PyLong_FromLong(42);
  PyModule_AddObject(m, "myValue", myValue);
  PyObject *myPyFun = PyCFunction_New(&myFunc_def, m);
  PyModule_AddObject(m, "myFunc", myPyFun);
  return 0;
}

PyObject *create(PyObject *spec, PyModuleDef *def)
{
  PyObject *res = PyObject_GetAttrString(spec, "origin");
  printf("%s\n", PyUnicode_AsUTF8(res));
  PyObject *m = PyModule_New("example");
  return m;
}

void freeModule(void *m){
    struct myData *myModData =
                      (struct myData *)PyModule_GetState(m);
    PyMem_Free(myModData);
}
PyModuleDef_Slot twoPhase[] = {
    {Py_mod_create, create},
    {Py_mod_exec, exec},
    {0, 0}};

static struct PyModuleDef myModuledef = {
    PyModuleDef_HEAD_INIT,
    "example",
    "C library to test API",
    sizeof(struct myData),
    NULL,
    twoPhase,
    NULL,
    NULL,
    freeModule};

PyMODINIT_FUNC PyInit_example(void)
{
  return PyModuleDef_Init(&myModuledef);
}
```

Summary

- A module behaves very much like a Python object in that it has attributes, which can be any other Python object.

- As well as using `PyMethodDef` to add attributes that are functions or methods, you can use `PyModule_AddObjectRef` and `PyModule_AddObject` to add objects directly.

- You can also create function attributes directly or using `PyMethodDef` and there are different possibilities for how parameters are passed.

- As well as C functions, you can also add Python functions defined in other modules as attributes.

- Single-phase module initialization is good enough for a range of tasks, but multi-phase initialization is required if you want a module to take advantage of multiprocessing.

- Multi-phase initialization provides the facilities needed to allocate memory on a per module basis. This allows different instances of the module to have their own data.

We have been making use of the `PyObject` struct since very early on – you can't really do without it. This is because in Python and in the C API everything is an object and in the case of the C API specifically a `PyObject`. However the real work is done not by `PyObject` but by `PyTypeObject`. It is more accurate to say that in the C API everything is a type object. So far we have been using predefined type objects, but if we want to create custom objects we have to look more closely at the `PyTypeObject`. Knowing how it works is not only useful in constructing new objects, but it also is the key to understanding how Python works. The `PyTypeObject` is at the core of the language and nearly everything in Python is based on it.

Structs As Objects In C

So far we have been using types that have been provided by Python. Now it is time to create a type in C and present it for use in Python. This isn't difficult, but it is intricate and very detailed.

In Python a type is almost synonymous with class. So far we have used `PyObject*` as a pointer to something we have referred to as a Python object. In fact the `PyObject` is a very simple `struct`:

```
typedef struct {
    Py_ssize_t ob_refcnt;
    PyTypeObject *ob_type;
}PyObject;
```

The first field is just a simple reference count – how many other objects hold a reference to the object. The second field is a pointer to the type object that provides the basic attributes for the object.

We have been using `PyObject` and many other similar objects from the first program, but you may not have noticed how it all works. If you have seen this technique before you can skip to the next section.

The main question to answer is, given there is a wide range of objects with far more fields than the PyObject struct, how is it that we can cast them all to PyObject?

Creating object hierarchies in C is all a matter of casting pointers to structs and this was discussed in detail in Chapter 1.

For example, suppose you have a simple struct of a two-dimensional point:

```
typedef struct {
  int x;
  int y:
}point2;
```

then you can extend this, "subclass" it, to create a three-dimensional point:

```
typedef struct {
  int x;
  int y;
  int z;
}point3;
```

You might be thinking in what sense is this subclassing as we just have two structs? Suppose you declare a pointer to a `point3` struct:

```
point3 *point3d;
```

now you can reference all its fields x,y and z. However if you cast it to a point2 pointer

```
point2 *point2d = (point2*) point3d;
```

then `point2d` references the same struct as `point3d`, but you can only access the x and y fields.

What is slightly more surprising is that you can use the definition of a smaller struct to define the larger subclass. For example:

```
typedef struct {
  point2 pbase;
  int z;
}point3;
```

This makes the first part of the struct into enough space for two `int`s and this means it can still be cast to a `point2` pointer. That is:

```
point2 *point2d = (point2*) point3d;
```

still works and you can use `point2d->x` and `point2d->y`. The advantage is not having to repeat the definition of point2 at the start of point3, but we now have to use `point3d->pbase ->x` and `point3d -> pbase -> y` to access the fields of the "base" struct.

The is one final technique that is worth pointing out. A struct can have a variable size by including an array declaration at the end with just one element. For example:

```
  int32_t x;
  int32_t y;
int32_t tail[1]
} pointVar;
```

This struct can be used to reference a block of memory that is larger than its basic definition which is 12 bytes.

The final array can be as large as the memory allocated to it. If you create a struct using:

```
pointVar *structP = (pointVar*)  malloc(sizeof(pointVar)
                                   + sizeof(int) * (10 - 1));
```

you can use `structP.tail` to reference the additional memory either by indexing, e.g. `structP.tail[4]`, or by casting the pointer to another type. Notice for C99 and later the array should be declared as `tail[]`. There are some restrictions, the array must be at the end of the struct and you cannot use the struct within other structs – the reason for both restrictions should be obvious.

These are the mechanisms used by the Python system to implement objects. The `PyObject` struct is at the top of the hierarchy and all other similar objects are structs that start off with the same fields as `PyObject` and then add their own. You can see that if this prescription is followed, any API object can be cast to a `PyObject`. For example, there is a type of object that has a variable size, a `PyVarObject` type. This starts off with the same two fields as `PyObject`, but adds a third, `ob_size`, field.

```
typedef struct {
    PyObject o_base;
    Py_ssize_t ob_size
}PyVarObject;
```

Clearly this can be referenced by a `PyObject` pointer but the first two fields are now `o_base.ob_refcnt` and `o_base.ob_type` within `PyVarObject`.

Although the fields are simple it is recommended that you don't access any of the standard fields directly. Instead there are a set of macros that let you work with the fields:

- `Py_ssize_t Py_REFCNT(PyObject *o)`
- `void Py_SET_REFCNT(PyObject *o, Py_ssize_t refcnt)`

- `PyTypeObject *Py_TYPE(PyObject *o)`
- `void Py_SET_TYPE(PyObject *o, PyTypeObject *type)`

- `Py_ssize_t Py_SIZE(PyVarObject *o)`
- `void Py_SET_SIZE(PyVarObject *o, Py_ssize_t size)`

The reason for using these macros is simply to allow changes to the structs to be made transparently to the end user.

There are also macros to define the start of the object stucts that you create:

- `PyObject_HEAD`
- `PyObject_VAR_HEAD`

and to initialize them:

- `PyObject_HEAD_INIT(type)`
- `PyVarObject_HEAD_INIT(type, size)`

In each case the reference count is automatically set to one.

The PyTypeObject

As already stated, every Python object struct starts with the fields:

```
typedef struct {
    Py_ssize_t ob_refcnt;
    PyTypeObject *ob_type;
}PyObject;
```

The first field, ob_refcnt, is almost trivial in that it is the count of the number of references there are to the object. If it is zero the object is removed from memory by the garbage collector. The second field, *ob_type, is where all the work is done. The PyTypeObject referenced by ob_type contains definitions for the basic behavior of the object. This struct is the way that Python implements objects and its use is responsible for much of the character of Python. It starts off with the same two fields that a PyObject does, i.e. it too is a PyObject, but then follows with lots of additional fields.

Every object has a reference to a PyTypeObject including PyTypeObject itself which has a reference to a built-in type object which defines PyTypeObject and references itself. If you think of PyTypeObject as a class, then its type object is a metaclass.

The key idea is that the type object has a large number of fields called slots that mostly define the standard "magic", dunder functions, so-called because of the double underscores surrounding them, that can be called on the object. For example, there is a field/slot called tp_name which stores a C string that gives the name of the type and this is returned when you use the object's __name__ method.

The tp_name slot isn't typical as most slots point at functions that implement a magic method. For example, tp_str stores a reference to a C function that implements the __str__ magic method, i.e. it returns a string representation of the object. Any slots that you don't want to use can be ignored and the corresponding object features will be unavailable.

Some slots are organized as sub-slots – these simply reference another structure which contains a group of slots concerned with a single protocol. For example, tp_as_sequence is a sub-slot which can be set to reference a PySequenceMethod struct which has slots for all of the functions needed to implement the sequence protocol. If an object isn't a sequence you can simply ignore the slot and the sub-slot.

Of course, slots can only be used to implement predefined attributes. For custom attributes there is a slot that defines a dict to be used to record additional custom attributes.

In general there are two structs that are associated with every object, `PyTypeObject` acts as the object's class and `PyObject` which defines the instance. For example, a Python integer is defined by a `PyTypeObject` called `PyLong_Type` and you can think of this as the class to use when you create an instance of a Python integer, so a `PyLongObject` struct is created when you want to reference a `PyLong_Type`. The `PyLongObject` struct holds all of the attributes that belong to the instance and `PyLong_Type` holds all of the attributes that belong to the class. There is only one `PyLong_Type` struct shared by all of the instances, but there are many `PyLongObject` structs one for each instance.

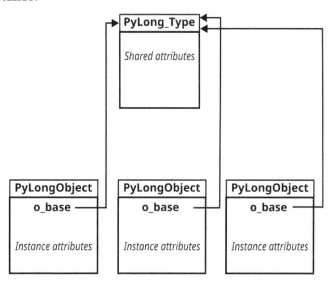

A First Custom Type

There are a great many slots that you can use to define a custom type and the problem is knowing where to start. The simplest solution is to find out about the slots that are necessary to create a basic custom type and then find out about the others as and when they are needed. The documentation contains a complete list and descriptions of each.

As `PyTypeObject` is an object, if we create a custom `PyTypeObject` it can be made an attribute of the module in the usual way. It also plays the role of a Python class and it can be used to create new instances of the type, but for the moment it is simpler to create a type that cannot be instantiated – our goal is the simplest possible example.

First we need a new `PyTypeObject` struct with just the slots we need filled in:

```
static PyTypeObject MyType1 = {
    PyVarObject_HEAD_INIT(NULL, 0)
    .tp_name = "example.myObject",
    .tp_doc = PyDoc_STR("My Custom object"),
    .tp_flags = Py_TPFLAGS_DEFAULT |
                        Py_TPFLAGS_DISALLOW_INSTANTIATION,
};
```

A `PyTypeObject` is a `Py_VarObject` so we have to initialize its first three fields using the `PyVarObject_HEAD_INIT` macro. Next we define its name, the doc string and use the flags slot to disable instantiation. Before we can use the new type it has to be made ready:

```
int res = PyType_Ready(&MyType1);
```

`PyType_Ready` sets the slots of the type appropriately using a number of different rules. It usually leaves slots that you have set unmodified, but there are combinations of slot values that force other slots to have a particular value. In many cases the default value of a slot is "inherited",

Now that `MyType1` is set correctly, it can be added to the module as an attribute:

```
PyModule_AddObject(m, "MyClass", (PyObject *)&MyType1);
```

The full program is:

```
#define PY_SSIZE_T_CLEAN
#include <Python.h>

static PyTypeObject MyType1 = {
    PyVarObject_HEAD_INIT(NULL, 0)
    .tp_name = "example.myObject",
    .tp_doc = PyDoc_STR("My Custom object"),
    .tp_flags = Py_TPFLAGS_DEFAULT |
                        Py_TPFLAGS_DISALLOW_INSTANTIATION,
};
static struct PyModuleDef myModule = {
    PyModuleDef_HEAD_INIT,
    "example",
    "C library to test API",
    -1,
    NULL};
PyMODINIT_FUNC PyInit_example(void)
{
  PyObject *m = PyModule_Create(&myModule);
  if (m == NULL)
    return NULL;
  int res = PyType_Ready(&MyType1);
  PyModule_AddObject(m, "MyClass", (PyObject *)&MyType1);
  return m;
}
```

No error handing is included and you should check that the `PyType_Ready` succeeds and decrements the reference count if `AddObject` fails.

If you compile this, the new class object can be used from Python:

```
import example
myclass=example.MyClass
print(myclass)
print(myclass.__dict__)
```

which displays:

```
<class 'example.myObject'>
{'__doc__': 'My Custom object'}
```

This indicates that we have a basic class object and its dict only contains the single key __doc__ set to the value supplied in the struct. It may not be much, but it demonstrates the basic idea.

This is also a static type, that is, the struct has been declared static rather than a heap type which is declared on the heap. Static types are limited to single inheritance, they are not mutable and they are shared across sub-interpreters. The fact that they are not mutable is their biggest drawback in that the user cannot dynamically add or remove attributes or change attributes defined on the class.

The class may be immutable, but any instances create from it can be mutable and this brings to the subject of how to create a class that can be instantiated.

Instantiation

A type that can be instantiated can be called. In Python this results in a call to a new function that returns a block of memory that is treated as a `PyObject` which means that it has at least a reference count and a type pointer. To enable this behavior we need to make several changes to the custom `PyTypeObject`:

```
static PyTypeObject MyType1 = {
    PyVarObject_HEAD_INIT(NULL, 0)
    .tp_name = "example.myObject",
    .tp_doc = PyDoc_STR("My Custom object"),
    .tp_flags = Py_TPFLAGS_DEFAULT,
    .tp_basicsize = sizeof(PyObject),
    .tp_itemsize = 0,
    .tp_new = PyType_GenericNew,
};
```

Notice that now we have removed the `Py_TPFLAGS_DISALLOW_INSTANTIATION` flag, we have set the size of the block of memory to return and have created a default `tp_new` function. The `PyType_GenericNew` simply returns a block of memory specified by `tp_basicsize` initialized so that its reference count is 1 and its type is set to `MyType1`. In this example `tp_basicsize` is set to the minimum `PyObject`. In general, instances can have a variable size and in this case the amount of memory allocated is `tp_basicsize * tp_itemsize`.

If you try this out:

```
my Inst=example.MyClass()
print(my Inst)
print(my Inst.__dir__())
print(my Inst.__sizeof__())
```

you will find that it works as expected:

```
<example.myObject object at 0x0000026437C541A0>
['__new__', '__doc__', '__repr__', '__hash__', '__str__',
'__getattribute__', '__setattr__', '__delattr__', '__lt__',
'__le__', '__eq__', '__ne__', '__gt__', '__ge__', '__init__',
'__reduce_ex__', '__reduce__', '__getstate__', '__subclasshook__',
'__init_subclass__', '__format__', '__sizeof__', '__dir__',
'__class__']
16
```

This may work, but it isn't much use as the new instance doesn't have any custom attributes – just the ones inherited from its basic class. Notice that by default the new instance doesn't have a __dict__ and this means you can't dynamically add attributes to the instance.

Although the modifications introduced are small, they are crucial and a full listing can be found on the book's webpage.

Adding Attributes To The Class

In Python we can add attributes to the class or to the instance – the class attributes are available to all its instances and the instance attributes are unique to the instance.

What happens when you get an attribute is that the instance dict is searched first, if there is one, and then the class dict is searched. If the attribute still isn't found then the dicts in the inheritance chain are searched. If the attribute is found, the value in the dict is returned. There is a modification to this algorithm that involves the use of "descriptors", see later, but this is the most basic implementation of attributes.

It should be obvious that attributes stored on the instance belong to the instance and can be different from other instances of the class. Attributes that are stored on the class are shared by all of the instances of the class that don't define their own version of the attribute. The general rule is that methods belong in the class so that they can be shared and data belongs in the instance so that they can be different from other instances.

Lets start by defining attributes on the class – i.e. the type object. You can do this in a number of ways but the most basic is to create and add the new attributes to a dict. For example, let's start with a simple data attribute:

```
PyMODINIT_FUNC PyInit_example(void)
{
  PyObject *m = PyModule_Create(&myModule);
  if (m == NULL)
    return NULL;
  PyObject *mydict = PyDict_New();
  PyObject *val = PyLong_FromLong(42);
  PyDict_SetItemString(mydict, "myValue", val);
  Py_DECREF(val);
  MyType1.tp_dict = mydict;
  int res = PyType_Ready(&MyType1);
  PyModule_AddObject(m, "MyClass", (PyObject *)&MyType1);
  return m;
}
```

Notice that the dict is created, initialized and then added to the type before we call PyType_Ready, This is the correct way to do the job and the documentation warns of directly manipulating the dict after the type has been created and is in use. If you add this to the earlier example you can try:

```
import example
print(example.MyClass.myValue)
example.MyClass.myValue=43
```

The first instruction displays 42 as you would expect, but the second fails because MyClass is immutable. If you try the same thing with an instance of the class you will still see 42 and any attempt to change the value results in the error that the attribute is read-only. They both fail, but for different reasons – the instance doesn't have a dict and so cannot support the attribute in read/write mode.

Adding a function attribute is only slightly more difficult. You first have to convert the C function to a Python object as explained in Chapter 10. The C function is simple and just prints something:

```
static PyObject *myFunc(PyObject *self, PyObject *args)
{
  printf("hello world\n");
  Py_RETURN_NONE;
}
```

To convert the C function to a Python object we need a PyMethodDef describing it:

```
static PyMethodDef myFunc_def = {
    "myFunc",
    myFunc,
    METH_VARARGS,
    "the doc string"};
```

Finally we can convert the C function to a Python object and add it to the dict:

```
PyObject *myPyFun = PyCFunction_New(&myFunc_def,
                                    (PyObject*)&MyType1);
PyDict_SetItemString(mydict,"myFunc",myPyFun);
```

The only problem is that we have to set "self" to something and in this case it seems reasonable to set it to the type, i.e. the class. If you add this to the previous example you can try it out:

```
example.MyClass.myFunc()
my Inst=example.MyClass()
myInst.myFunc()
```

In both cases you will see "hello world" displayed. The attempt to call myFunc on the instance is automatically passed to the class. Notice that in both cases self is myType1 – we still have to find out how to implement a true method that is bound to the instance.

Although the modifications introduced are small a full listing can be found on the book's webpage.

Instance Attributes

Adding a simple attribute to the class is easy and the instance gets to make use of them via the usual Python resolution mechanism. When you try to use an attribute on an instance the instance's dict is searched first and if it isn't found the class's dict is searched and so on up the inheritance chain. At the moment the problem is that the instance we create doesn't have a dict and so it can't host instance attributes.

The solution is, of course, to give it a dict so it can record instance attributes. This turns out to be easier than you might have imagined. If you provide space for a pointer in the instance then the system will create and manage a dict for you. To provide additional space for storage in the instance we need to move to using a custom struct to define the instance, for example:

```
typedef struct
{
  PyObject_HEAD
  PyObject *dict;
} MyObject;
```

Now we can use:

```
    .tp_basicsize = sizeof(MyObject),
```

to set the size of the block of memory returned when an instance is created.

To make the system use the space allocated for the pointer we have to set the .tp_dictoffset slot to the offset from the start of the memory block of the pointer we want the system to use. This is most easily done using the offsetof function which is defined in stddef.h. You might need to add:

```
#include <stddef.h>
```

Now setting .tp_dictoffset is easy:

```
.tp_dictoffset = offsetof(MyObject, dict),
```

With these two simple changes you now have the ability to use instance attributes. For example, you can now use:

```
myInst.myValue = 43
print(myInst.myValue)
```

and you will see 43 displayed, i.e. the myValue attribute is no longer read-only.

You can also create new attributes dynamically:

```
myInst.myVal1 = 42
print(myInst.myVal1)
```

and you will see 42 displayed and myVal1 is now an attribute of the instance.

If you create additional instances then each one inherits the attributes from the class and these are added to the dict when it is first assigned to and so becomes an instance attribute. This is how a full Python instance behaves, although there is an alternative way to create instance attributes based on the use of descriptors, see later.

Again, although the modifications introduced are small a full listing can be found on the book's webpage.

Instance Methods – new and init

There are a number of ways of implementing instance methods, but it is worth knowing how to do it the way that pure Python does the job. What we have to do is create a method that automatically sets the self parameter to the instance and make this method an instance attribute. This part is relatively easy as there is a function which changes the call to a function into a bound method:

```
PyObject *PyInstanceMethod_New(PyObject *func)
```

The problem we have is that we have to create the method and add it to the instance's dict when the instance is created. At the moment we are making use of a system-supplied new function. This simply creates and returns a block of memory large enough to store the instance. In fact, the C API supports both a custom new and a custom init function. As in the case of pure Python, the new function is responsible for creating the instance and the init is used to add instance attributes. Usually instance attributes are thought to be data, but this is only because the system adds method objects for you.

This is a complicated idea when you first meet it, so it is worth being more precise. The idea is that the class that the instance derives from has functions of the form:

```
function(self, args)
```

These are the usual functions that you create to be used as methods for the instances, but when you call them as methods you don't supply the `self` parameter:

```
myInst.method(args)
```

as `my Inst` is automatically set as the `self` parameter. The way that this works is that the system converts the functions in the class into methods by binding `self` to the instance:

```
method = function(self=instance, args)
```

This allows you to write

```
myInst.method(args)
```

and have it converted into a call:

```
function(my Inst,args)
```

Notice the distinction between the function that requires `self` to be specified and the method derived from it which doesn't.

The instance doesn't get a local copy of the function, just a pointer to the function in the class. That is, the method just changes how the function is called and this is reasonably efficient.

To make this conversion of a function into a method we need to implement our own custom init that adds both any instance data attributes and any method attributes.

In this case we don't actually need a custom new, but it is instructive to create one:

```
static PyObject * Custom_new(PyTypeObject *type,
                             PyObject *args, PyObject *kwds)
{
    MyObject *self;
    self = (MyObject *) type->tp_alloc(type, 0);
    return (PyObject *) self;
}
```

The only thing that the new function has to do is allocate enough space for the instance and that's what the default `tp_alloc` function does. A pointer to this block of memory is returned as `self` which is in turn passed to the custom init function so that attributes can be added and the instance generally prepared.

178

In our case we are interested in setting up just a method attribute. The function that defines the method is trivial:

```
static PyObject *myFunc(MyObject *self, PyObject *args)
{
  printf("hello world\n");
  Py_RETURN_NONE;
};
```

As this needs to be converted from a C function into a PyCFunction, it also needs a PyMethodDef:

```
static PyMethodDef myFunc_def = {
    "myFunc",
    (PyCFunction) myFunc,
    METH_VARARGS,
    "the doc string"};
```

The custom init can now be put together:

```
static int Custom_init(MyObject *self, PyObject *args,
                                       PyObject *kwds)
{
  PyObject *myPyFunc = PyCFunction_New(&myFunc_def,
                                       (PyObject*) self);
  PyObject *myPyMethod = PyInstanceMethod_New(myPyFunc);
  int res= PyObject_SetAttrString((PyObject*)self, "MyMethod",
                                       myPyMethod);
  return 0;
}
```

You can see that all this does is create a PyCFunction from the C function and then convert this into a method which is bound to the new instance. At the time that the custom init is run, self is set to point at the instance and so the method is indeed bound to the instance. Notice the way that SetAttrString is used to add the method to the instance's dict. We also have to change the type object to make use of our Custom_new and Custom_init:

```
    .tp_new = Custom_new,
    .tp_init=(initproc) Custom_init,
```

The complete listing, including the attributes added in previous sections is:

```c
#define PY_SSIZE_T_CLEAN
#include <Python.h>
#include <stddef.h>
typedef struct
{
  PyObject_HEAD
      PyObject *dict;
} MyObject;

static PyObject *myFunc(PyObject *self, PyObject *args)
{
  printf("hello world\n");
  Py_RETURN_NONE;
}

static PyMethodDef myFunc_def = {
    "myFunc",
    myFunc,
    METH_VARARGS,
    "the doc string"};

static PyObject *Custom_new(PyTypeObject *type,
                            PyObject *args, PyObject *kwds)
{
  MyObject *self;
  self = (MyObject *)type->tp_alloc(type, 0);
  return (PyObject *)self;
}

static int Custom_init(MyObject *self,
                       PyObject *args, PyObject *kwds)
{
  PyObject *myPyFunc = PyCFunction_New(&myFunc_def,
                                        (PyObject *)self);
  PyObject *myPyMethod = PyInstanceMethod_New(myPyFunc);
  int res = PyObject_SetAttrString((PyObject *)self,
                                    "MyMethod", myPyMethod);
  return 0;
}
static PyTypeObject MyType1 = {
    PyVarObject_HEAD_INIT(NULL, 0)
    .tp_name = "example.myObject",
    .tp_doc = PyDoc_STR("My Custom object"),
    .tp_flags = Py_TPFLAGS_DEFAULT,
    .tp_basicsize = sizeof(MyObject),
    .tp_itemsize = 0,
    .tp_dictoffset = offsetof(MyObject, dict),
    .tp_new = Custom_new,
    .tp_init = (initproc)Custom_init,
};
```

```
static struct PyModuleDef myModule = {
    PyModuleDef_HEAD_INIT,
    "example",
    "C library to test API",
    -1,
    NULL};

PyMODINIT_FUNC PyInit_example(void)
{
  PyObject *m = PyModule_Create(&myModule);
  if (m == NULL)
    return NULL;
  PyObject *mydict = PyDict_New();
  PyObject *val = PyLong_FromLong(42);
  PyDict_SetItemString(mydict, "myValue", val);
  Py_DECREF(val);
  PyObject *myPyFun = PyCFunction_New(&myFunc_def,
                                      (PyObject *)&MyType1);
  PyDict_SetItemString(mydict, "myFunc", myPyFun);
  MyType1.tp_dict = mydict;
  int res = PyType_Ready(&MyType1);
  PyModule_AddObject(m, "MyClass", (PyObject *)&MyType1);
  return m;
}
```
If you try this out:
```
myinst=example.MyClass()
myinst.MyMethod()
```
You will see "hello world". This doesn't really prove that the method is bound to the instance, as it would print the message no matter what it was bound to. However, if you add an instance data attribute as described earlier and if you modify the function to access it you will find that it uses the value corresponding to the instance.

Notice that this way of creating methods doesn't quite follow what happens in pure Python. In this case the methods are defined as function on the class and when an instance is created all of these functions are wrapped as bound methods and installed into the instance's dict. It is not difficult to see that you could do the same in the C API. For example, if you add the method to the type's dict:
```
  PyObject *mydict = PyDict_New();
  PyObject *myPyFun = PyCFunction_New(&myFunc_def,
                                      (PyObject *)&MyType1);
  PyDict_SetItemString(mydict, "MyMethod", myPyFun);
  MyType1.tp_dict = mydict;
```

Then the custom `init` function can use this as the basis for its instance method:

```
static int Custom_init(MyObject *self, PyObject *args,
                                          PyObject *kwds)
{
  PyObject* myPyFunc=PyDict_GetItemString(
                ((PyObject*)self)->ob_type->tp_dict,"MyMethod");
  PyObject *myPyMethod = PyInstanceMethod_New(myPyFunc);
  int res = PyObject_SetAttrString((PyObject *)self,
                                    "MyMethod", myPyMethod);
  res = PyObject_SetAttrString((PyObject *)self, "myValue",
                                    PyLong_FromLong(42));
  return 0;
}
```

Of course, you could scan through the type's dict for all of the callable attributes and convert them to instance methods. However, this doesn't seem necessary as you are creating the type and hence already know the list of functions to turn into instance methods.

The suggestion is that you use `new` to create and initialize things that are immutable and use `init` to create and initialize things which are mutable. The reason is that derived classes often override the `init` function in the base class, see Chapter 13.

Descriptors

It is very well worth knowing how to directly add attributes and methods to the instance, but this is not how the job is usually done. Building the class dict an attribute at a time is perfectly reasonable, but there is a much easier way to do the same job and this brings us to the more sophisticated way of adding attributes - descriptors.

A descriptor is simply an object with a `get`, `set` and `del` method. The purpose of the methods is to get, set and delete an attribute.

The simple attributes we have been implemented have been dictionary-based. For example, to get a value the instance's and then the type's dictionary (including any types in the inheritance chain) are searched for the attribute and when it is found the value is returned. However, if the value is a descriptor object the `get` method is called and the value it returns is the value of the attribute. The same idea works for setting a value except that the `set` method is called if found.

What is important about descriptors is that they can be used to implement instance attributes without having to create a dict for the instance. The reason that this is possible is that when the `get` and `set` methods are called they are automatically provided with the instance set as `self`.

The C API has some functions that make creating descriptors for data attributes and methods very simple. There are three descriptor functions:

- PyObject *PyDescr_NewGetSet(PyTypeObject *type,
                                     struct PyGetSetDef *getset)
- PyObject *PyDescr_NewMethod(PyTypeObject *type,
                                     struct PyMethodDef *meth)
- PyObject *PyDescr_NewMember(PyTypeObject *type,
                                     struct PyMemberDef *meth)

The NewGetSet function is discussed later. The NewMember and NewMethod functions create descriptors for data attributes and methods respectively. We have met PyMethodDef previously and the NewMethod function simply adds the method descriptor to the class.

The NewMember function uses a new struct to describe the member and PyMemberDef is:

```
typedef{
  const char *name
  int type
  Py_ssize_t offset
  int flags
  const char *doc
}PyMemberDef
```

The idea is that the data for the member is stored in the instance as a C type at a specified offset from the start of the struct. The type field specifies the C type and what Python type it should be converted to. It can be any of:

C Type	Python Type
T_SHORT	short
T_INT	int
T_LONG	long
T_FLOAT	float
T_DOUBLE	double
T_STRING	const char *
T_OBJECT	PyObject *
T_OBJECT_EX	PyObject *
T_CHAR	char
T_BYTE	char
T_UBYTE	unsigned char
T_UINT	unsigned int
T_USHORT	unsigned short
T_ULONG	unsigned long
T_BOOL	char
T_LONGLONG	long long
T_ULONGLONG	unsigned long long
T_PYSSIZET	Py_ssize_t

183

Notice that all of these constants are being upgraded (Python 3.13) to have a PY at the start but the old versions should be supported for the foreseeable future.

The flags field can be 0 for read/write access or READONLY for read-only access. Using T_STRING for type implies READONLY. T_STRING data is interpreted as UTF-8. Notice that T_OBJECT and T_OBJECT_EX types give you a way of using Python objects and they are the only members can be deleted. Use T_OBJECT_EX as it returns an exception if the member is NULL.

Notice that this goes beyond the simple idea of a descriptor in pure Python as a get/set/del object. A C API descriptor also provides automatic conversion between C types and Python types, which is very helpful. You always have a choice of using a C type or a Python type in an extension class. For example, to implement a simple count, you could use a C int as a T_INT or you could use a T_OBJECT_EX and a Python int object. In nearly all cases using a C data type is more efficient and easier.

A simple example of adding a method and an integer member should make things clear. First we need a struct to define the instance:

```
typedef struct
{
  PyObject_HEAD
  int myVal;
} MyObject;
```

The instance is a PyObject with a single additional int field. The method to be added is defined by the C function:

```
static PyObject *myFunc(MyObject *self, PyObject *args)
{
  printf("%d\n", self->myVal);
  printf("hello world\n");
  Py_RETURN_NONE;
};
```

This simply displays the current value of myVal as a C type and a message to show it has been called. The member and method definitions are:

```
static PyMemberDef myMemberdef = {
    "MyVar",
    T_INT,
    offsetof(MyObject, myVal),
    0,
    "MyInstanceAttr"};

static PyMethodDef myFunc_def = {
    "myFunc",
    (PyCFunction)myFunc,
    METH_VARARGS,
    "the doc string"};
```

All that remains is to add these definitions to the class and this is done by adding the descriptors to the class dict just before the call to PyType_Ready:

```
PyObject *mydict=PyDict_New();
PyObject *myMethodDesc = PyDescr_NewMethod(&MyType1,
                                                &myFunc_def);
int res = PyDict_SetItemString(mydict, "MyMethod", myMethodDesc);
PyObject *myMemberDesc = PyDescr_NewMember(&MyType1,
                                                &myMemberdef);
res = PyDict_SetItemString(mydict, "MyVar", myMemberDesc);
MyType2.tp_dict=mydict;
res = PyType_Ready(&MyType1);
```

This is the minimum required to make the descriptors work. The full listing is:

```
#define PY_SSIZE_T_CLEAN
#include <Python.h>
#include <stddef.h>
#include "structmember.h"

typedef struct
{
  PyObject_HEAD
  int myVal;
} MyObject;

static PyObject *myFunc(MyObject *self, PyObject *args)
{
  printf("%d\n", self->myVal);
  printf("hello world\n");
  Py_RETURN_NONE;
};


static PyMemberDef myMemberdef = {
    "MyVar",
    T_INT,
    offsetof(MyObject, myVal),
    0,
    "MyInstanceAttr"};

static PyMethodDef myFunc_def = {
    "myFunc",
    (PyCFunction)myFunc,
    METH_VARARGS,
    "the doc string"};
```

```
static PyTypeObject MyType1 = {
    .ob_base = PyVarObject_HEAD_INIT(NULL, 0)
    .tp_name = "example.myObject",
    .tp_doc = PyDoc_STR("My Custom object"),
    .tp_flags = Py_TPFLAGS_DEFAULT,
    .tp_basicsize = sizeof(MyObject),
    .tp_itemsize = 0,
    .tp_new =PyType_GenericNew,
};

static struct PyModuleDef myModule = {
    PyModuleDef_HEAD_INIT,
    "example",
    "C library to test API",
    -1,
    NULL};

PyMODINIT_FUNC PyInit_example(void)
{
  PyObject *m = PyModule_Create(&myModule);
  if (m == NULL)
    return NULL;

  PyObject *mydict=PyDict_New();
  PyObject *myMethodDesc = PyDescr_NewMethod(&MyType1,
                                             &myFunc_def);
  int res = PyDict_SetItemString(mydict, "MyMethod", myMethodDesc);

  PyObject *myMemberDesc = PyDescr_NewMember(&MyType1,
                                             &myMemberdef);
  res = PyDict_SetItemString(mydict, "MyVar", myMemberDesc);
  MyType1.tp_dict=mydict;
  res = PyType_Ready(&MyType1);
  PyModule_AddObject(m, "MyClass", (PyObject *)&MyType1);
  return m;
}
```

If you try this out you will find that instances have an attribute called MyVar that is specific to the instance and a method which displays the instance's value of MyVar. Notice that you cannot use MyVar as an attribute of the class as it is immutable and descriptors behave differently for class and instance.

Easy Descriptor Attributes

The simplest way to provide an instance with attributes and methods is to use a descriptor – especially because the C API provides a way to automatically create them that is similar to adding functions to a module

The PyTypeObject has two slots that can be used to set an array of member and method definitions. When you call PyType_Ready each of these arrays is processed and member, i.e. non-function, attributes and methods are added to the class dict as descriptors. This makes it trivial to add instance attributes. All you have to do is:

1. Make sure that you allocate fields in the struct that defines the instance for all of the data attributes you want to add.
2. Define C functions for all of the methods you want to add.
3. Create `Attribute` and `Method` arrays.
4. Set `tp_members` and `tp_methods` to the arrays.
5. Call `PyType_Ready`.
6. Create instances and use the methods and attributes.

For example, to set up the same method and member that we used in the previous example we already have the appropriate fields and C functions. The attribute and method arrays are:

```
static PyMemberDef myMemberdef[] = {
    { "MyVar",T_INT,offsetof(MyObject, myVal),0,"MyInstanceAttr"},
    {NULL}
  };

static PyMethodDef myMethodDef[] = {
  {"MyMethod",(PyCFunction)myFunc,METH_VARARGS,"the doc string"},
  {NULL}
  };
```

Notice that these are null-terminated arrays, not just single structs as used in the previous example. Now we can set the type to reference these arrays:

```
static PyTypeObject MyType1 = {
    .ob_base = PyVarObject_HEAD_INIT(NULL, 0)
    .tp_name = "example.myObject",
    .tp_doc = PyDoc_STR("My Custom object"),
    .tp_flags = Py_TPFLAGS_DEFAULT,
    .tp_basicsize = sizeof(MyObject),
    .tp_itemsize = 0,
    .tp_new = PyType_GenericNew,
    .tp_members = myMemberdef,
    .tp_methods = myMethodDef,
};
```

No other changes to the example are required, apart from removing the lines that manually create and add the descriptors. A full listing of the modified program can be found on the book's webpage at www.iopress.info. The modified program works exactly the same as the previous example.

It is important to know how to manually add attributes both to the class and the instance, but using an array of descriptors is simple and efficient. It is the way to do the job unless you need something special. Of course, you can use the custom new and init function to set the C types to correct initial values and you can process the arguments of the methods in the usual way.

Get and Set Attributes

What if you want to make use of the full get/set abilities of a descriptor? When you use a member or a method the get/set function are generated for you. If you want to create your own the solution is to use the `PyGetSetDef` array and the `.tp_getset` slot. The `PyGetSetDef` array is made up of structs with the following fields:

Field	Type	
name	const char *	attribute name
get	getter	C get function
set	setter	C set function to set or delete the attribute, if omitted
doc	const char *	optional docstring
closure	void *	optional pointer, providing additional data

The only one that needs any explanation is the `closure` field. This could be implemented as a closure, i.e. a tuple of cell objects, but equally it could be any data or function that helps determine the value to be returned or set. In most simple cases it is set to `NULL`.

The getter and setter functions have the signatures:

```
typedef PyObject *getter(PyObject *self, void *closure);
typedef int setter(PyObject *self, PyObject *value, void *closure);
```

The only real problem in using custom `get` and `set` is keeping track of references. For example, adding a simple property `PyObject*` attribute is very easy:

```
static PyGetSetDef myGetSetDef[] = {
    {"myProperty", (getter)getVal, (setter)setVal,
                                "Example get set", NULL},
    {NULL}};
```

Now all we need are implementations of the functions. The `get` is very easy:

```
static PyObject *getVal(MyObject *self, void *extra)
{
  return Py_NewRef(self->myProp);
}
```

In this case we simply return the value stored in `PyObject *myProp`. We need to increment its reference count and this is most easily done using the `Py_NewRef(ob)` macro which adds one to the reference count and returns ob.

The set is slightly more complicated because we have to safely decrement the reference count of the existing value and increment the reference count of the new value:

```
int setVal(MyObject *self, PyObject *val, void *extra)
{
  PyObject *temp=self->myProp;
  self->myProp = val;
  Py_XINCREF(val);
  Py_DECREF(temp);
  return 0;
}
```

As always, to avoid triggering the removal of the existing value before the new value is stored, we need to take a temporary copy of the reference and decrement it later. The same action can be achieved using the Py_XSETREF macro which makes a copy and decrements the reference count in the same way:

```
int setVal(MyObject *self, PyObject *val, void *extra)
{
    Py_XSETREF(self->myProp,Py_XNewRef(val));
    return 0;
}
```

To make it all work we need to add a myProp field to the instance struct:

```
typedef struct
{
  PyObject_HEAD
  PyObject *myProp;
} MyObject;
```

and update the type object:

```
static PyTypeObject MyType1 = {
    .ob_base = PyVarObject_HEAD_INIT(NULL, 0)
    .tp_name = "example.myObject",
    .tp_doc = PyDoc_STR("My Custom object"),
    .tp_flags = Py_TPFLAGS_DEFAULT,
    .tp_basicsize = sizeof(MyObject),
    .tp_itemsize = 0,
    .tp_new = PyType_GenericNew,
    .tp_getset = myGetSetDef,
};
```

The complete program is:

```c
#define PY_SSIZE_T_CLEAN
#include <Python.h>
#include <stddef.h>
#include "structmember.h"

typedef struct
{
 PyObject_HEAD
 PyObject *myProp;
} MyObject;

static PyObject *getVal(MyObject *self, void *extra)
{
 return Py_NewRef(self->myProp);
}

int setVal(MyObject *self, PyObject *val, void *extra)
{
 Py_XSETREF(self->myProp, Py_XNewRef(val));
 return 0;
}

static PyGetSetDef myGetSetDef[] = {
 {"myProperty", (getter)getVal, (setter)setVal,
 "Example get set", NULL},
 {NULL}};

static PyTypeObject MyType1 = {
 .ob_base = PyVarObject_HEAD_INIT(NULL, 0)
 .tp_name = "example.myObject",
 .tp_doc = PyDoc_STR("My Custom object"),
 .tp_flags = Py_TPFLAGS_DEFAULT,
 .tp_basicsize = sizeof(MyObject),
 .tp_itemsize = 0,
 .tp_new = PyType_GenericNew,
 .tp_getset = myGetSetDef,
};

static struct PyModuleDef myModule = {
    PyModuleDef_HEAD_INIT,
    "example",
    "C library to test API",
    -1,
    NULL};
```

```
PyMODINIT_FUNC PyInit_example(void)
{
  PyObject *m = PyModule_Create(&myModule);
  if (m == NULL)
    return NULL;

  int res = PyType_Ready(&MyType1);
  PyModule_AddObject(m, "MyClass", (PyObject *)&MyType1);
  return m;
}
```

You can try it out using:

```
import example
myInst=example.MyClass()
myInst.myProperty=42
print(myInst.myProperty)
```

Of course, there is little point in implementing attributes using get and set unless you are going to do something additional to the values involved, but that is very specific to the problem you are trying to solve.

Summary

- Python objects are associated with two C structs, `PyTypeObject` and `PyObject`.

- The `PyTypeObject` stores all of the attributes that are part of the class and every instance of the class.

- The `PyObject` stores all of the attributes that are specific to the instance.

- To create a custom type all you have to do is create an instance of `PyTypeObject`, set the slots you need to use and then call `PyType_Ready` to set the rest.

- If you create a custom type that can be instantiated, you also need to define an extension of `PyObject` to represent each instance.

- Adding attributes to the type/class is just a matter of setting up a dict with the appropriate key value pairs.

- A static type is immutable and can only be used in single inheritance.

- To add attributes to an instance you have to create a dict as an attribute of the `PyObject` to store them.

- When an instance is created the new function is called to create the `PyObject` and the init function is called to customize it.

- To add methods to an instance you have to convert a function which is defined as an attribute of the type into a method and add it to the instance.

- Methods are added to the instance in the init function.

- You can add instance attributes more easily using descriptors. There is a separate structure for methods and members.

- Descriptors also support get/set properties as instance attributes.

Chapter 13

Advanced Types

Now that we know the basics of creating type objects and adding methods and attributes it is time to look at some more subtle and advanced ideas. These are not difficult, but they are isolated topics that are hard to put together to form an overall impression of how you should create and work with type objects.

Garbage Collection

So far we have ignored any issues of garbage collection, GC, other than simple reference counting. The cost of not implementing GC correctly is a memory leak. How important this is depends on how often the memory is allocated. Python has the concept of "immortal" objects which persist for the entire life of the program. For example, any static type objects you create are immortal, but any instances they are used to create are not. In general, any static object is immortal and not subject to GC of any kind. You can think of a one-off memory leak as just creating an immortal object by accident, or perhaps on purpose. However, if you are creating and destroying lots of objects then the accumulated memory used up will be a serious problem.

The simplest form of GC is pure reference counting. When an object's reference count is reduced to zero it is removed. Every time you call Py_DECREF() and Py_XDECREF() to decrement a reference count, the resulting value is checked and, if it is zero, the object's destructor, as indicated by the tp_dealloc slot, is called. Notice that the destructor is called at once and before the macro returns. Exactly how the destructor should free the memory previously allocated depends on how the object was constructed. The simplest case is if the instance doesn't reference any Python objects:

```
static void Custom_dealloc(CustomObject *self)
{
    Py_TYPE(self)->tp_free((PyObject *) self);
}
```

which simply calls the tp_free slot which is automatically set to PyObject_Del() if the object was created using either PyObject_New or PyObject_NewVar. This frees the block of memory that was allocated when the instance was created.

For example:

```
#define PY_SSIZE_T_CLEAN
#include <Python.h>
#include <stddef.h>
#include "structmember.h"

typedef struct
{
    PyObject_HEAD int myVal;
} MyObject;

static void Custom_dealloc(MyObject *self)
{
    printf("destructor called\n");
    Py_TYPE(self)->tp_free((PyObject *)self);
}

static PyObject *myFunc(MyObject *self, PyObject *args)
{
    printf("%d\n", self->myVal);
    printf("hello world\n");
    Py_RETURN_NONE;
};

static PyMemberDef myMemberdef[] = {
    {"MyVar", T_INT, offsetof(MyObject, myVal), 0,
                                    "MyInstanceAttr"},
    {NULL}};

static PyMethodDef myMethodDef[] = {
    {"MyMethod", (PyCFunction)myFunc, METH_VARARGS,
                                    "the doc string"},
    {NULL}};

static PyTypeObject MyType1 = {
    .ob_base = PyVarObject_HEAD_INIT(NULL, 0)
                    .tp_name = "example.myObject",
    .tp_doc = PyDoc_STR("My Custom object"),
    .tp_flags = Py_TPFLAGS_DEFAULT,
    .tp_basicsize = sizeof(MyObject),
    .tp_itemsize = 0,
    .tp_new = PyType_GenericNew,
    .tp_members = myMemberdef,
    .tp_methods = myMethodDef,
    .tp_dealloc = (destructor)Custom_dealloc,
};
```

```
static struct PyModuleDef myModule = {
    PyModuleDef_HEAD_INIT,
    "example",
    "C library to test API",
    -1,
    NULL};
```

```
PyMODINIT_FUNC PyInit_example(void)
{
    PyObject *m = PyModule_Create(&myModule);
    if (m == NULL)
            return NULL;

    int res = PyType_Ready(&MyType1);
    PyModule_AddObject(m, "MyClass", (PyObject *)&MyType1);
    return m;
}
```

If you try this out with:

```
import example
myinst1=example.MyClass()
myinst1.MyVar=42
print(myinst1.MyVar)
myInst1=None
```

you will see 42 and destructor called. Notice that you don't have to worry about the attribute method as this is actually part of the class. Similarly you don't have to worry about myVal as this is a C type and destroyed along with the struct when the memory is freed.

However, if there are fields that refer to Python objects then you do have to decrement their reference count so that they will be garbage-collected if their reference count falls to zero. For example, it the object struct is:

```
typedef struct
{
  PyObject_HEAD
  int myVal;
  PyObject *myAttr;
} MyObject;
```

the dealloc function should be:

```
static void Custom_dealloc(MyObject *self)
{
  printf("destructor called\n");
  Py_CLEAR(self->myAttr);
  Py_TYPE(self)->tp_free((PyObject *)self);
}
```

The Py_CLEAR macro decrements the object reference count and removes the reference by setting it to NULL.

If you do reference any "atomic" Python objects such as integers, floats, strings etc, in fact anything that can't reference another Python object, then decrementing their reference counts is usually enough.

All of the examples given in the previous chapter should have had a destructor defined to work correctly with the GC.

Reference Cycles

All that really matters is that when the object is no longer required its reference count is decremented to zero and hence the object's destructor is called and it frees all of the memory used by the instance and decrements the reference count of any object that the instance referenced. Unfortunately this isn't always sufficient. For example, suppose we change MyObject to include a PytObject field:

```
typedef struct
{
  PyObject_HEAD
  int myVal;
  PyObject *myAttr;
} MyObject;
```

and add this to the MemberDef struct:

```
static PyMemberDef myMemberdef[] = {
    {"MyVar", T_INT, offsetof(MyObject, myVal), 0,
                                    "MyInstanceAttr"},
    {"MyAttr", T_OBJECT_EX, offsetof(MyObject, myAttr), 0,
                                    "MyInstandeAttr"},
    {NULL}};
```

If you now try the following program:

```
myinst1=example.MyClass()
myinst1.MyAttr=myInst1
myInst1=None
print("end")
while True:
    pass
```

you will discover that the destructor isn't called. If you interrupt the while loop you will then see the destructor called before the interpreter stops running.

The problem is the self-reference which means that even if nothing else in the program references myInst1 and thus it is effectively unreachable, it still has a reference count of 1 and so isn't removed.

Reference counting doesn't work when there are chains of references that form a loop – a reference cycle. The reason is exactly the same as the simple example, all non-loop references to the objects can be removed and thus the objects can be unreachable, but their reference count isn't zero.

Weak References

One solution to this sort of problem is to use a weak reference. A weak reference works in the same way as a reference, but it doesn't increase the reference count of the object. You can make your extension class support weak references by adding a field:

```
typedef struct
{
  PyObject_HEAD int myVal;
  PyObject *myAttr;
  PyObject *weaklist;
} MyObject;
```

and setting a slot:

```
    .tp_weaklistoffset = offsetof(MyObject,weaklist),
```

Having made these changes you can try:

```
import example
import weakref
myInst1=example.MyClass()
myInst1.MyAttr=weakref.ref(myInst1)
myInst1=None
print("end")
while True:
    pass
```

and you will see the destructor called before the `while` loop. A weak self-reference doesn't affect reference counting.

Although the modifications introduced are small, a full listing can be found on the book's webpage.

Cyclic Garbage Collection

A weak reference isn't really the solution to the problem as it doesn't stop the system from creating reference loops. To quote the documentation:

> "One could think that cycles are uncommon, but the truth is that many internal references needed by the interpreter create cycles everywhere."

What this means is, that if your extension class has fields that can be used to reference a general `PyObject` or any object that can reference an object, you should assume that cycles can form.

The solution to the problem is to modify your extension class so that Python's GC can attempt to find cycles and remove the class if it has no other references.

To make a class take part in GC you have to set `Py_TPFLAGS_HAVE_GC` in the `tp_flags` slot. Once you do this the object has to use `PyObject_GC_New` or `PyObject_GC_NewVar` to create the class and you need to call `PyObject_GC_Track()` to add the object to the GC.

If you are using the supplied `PyType_GenericNew` the correct allocation function is used automatically and `GC_Track` is called.

The destructor also has to call `PyObject_GC_UnTrack()` and the allocated memory has to be released using `PyObject_GC_Del()`.

The documentation makes it sound as if this is all you have to do, but there are two more requirements. You have to define the `tp_clear` slot as a function to safely decrement all of the objects referenced by the fields of the object and you have to define the `tp_traverse` slot to define which fields need to be included in the search for cycles. In both cases you most likely have to include all of the fields that can reference Python objects unless they are "atomic" and cannot host references to other Python objects.

To convert the previous example to full GC we first need to define the destructor:

```
static void Custom_dealloc(MyObject *self)
{
  printf("destructor called\n");
  PyObject *error_type,*error_value, *error_traceback;
  PyErr_Fetch(&error_type, &error_value, &error_traceback);
  PyObject_GC_UnTrack(self);
  Py_TYPE(self)->tp_clear((PyObject *)self);
  PyObject_GC_Del(self);
  PyErr_Restore(error_type, error_value, error_traceback);
}
```

You can see that this is slightly more complicated than promised because we need to save any exceptions that have been raised and restore them after removing the object. Apart from this, you can see that we have a call to `Untrack` and one to `GC_Del`. In a more complex example there may be C memory allocations to free as well as Python ones. We also call `tp_clear` to decrement the reference count of each of the attributes.

The clear function simply applies the `Py_CLEAR` macro to each of the fields that reference Python objects:

```
static int Custom_clear(MyObject *self)
{
  printf("clear called\n");

  Py_CLEAR(self->myAttr);
  return 0;
}
```

The clear macro safely decrements the reference count of the object.

The traverse function is the most mysterious, but you simply have to use the PyVISIT macro to apply the supplied visit function to each of the fields that could be involved in a reference cycle.

```
static int Custom_traverse(MyObject *self, visitproc visit,
                                              void *arg)
{
  printf("traverse called\n");
  Py_VISIT(self->myAttr);
  return 0;
}
```

Notice that a printf instruction has been included so you can see how the GC proceeds.

With these functions defined we now simply have to set the appropriate slots in the type object. The full listing is:

```
#define PY_SSIZE_T_CLEAN
#include <Python.h>
#include <stddef.h>
#include "structmember.h"
typedef struct
{
  PyObject_HEAD int myVal;
  PyObject *myAttr;
} MyObject;

static void Custom_dealloc(MyObject *self)
{
  printf("destructor called\n");
  PyObject *error_type,*error_value, *error_traceback;
  PyErr_Fetch(&error_type, &error_value, &error_traceback);
  PyObject_GC_UnTrack(self);
  Py_TYPE(self)->tp_clear((PyObject *)self);
  PyObject_GC_Del(self);
  PyErr_Restore(error_type, error_value, error_traceback);
}

static int Custom_clear(MyObject *self)
{
  printf("clear called\n");
  Py_CLEAR(self->myAttr);
  return 0;
}

static int Custom_traverse(MyObject *self, visitproc visit,
                                              void *arg)
{
  printf("traverse called\n");
  Py_VISIT(self->myAttr);
  return 0;
}
```

```c
static int Custom_init(MyObject *self, PyObject *args,
                                         PyObject *kwds)
{
  self->myVal = 0;
  self->myAttr = Py_None;
  Py_XINCREF(Py_None);
  return 0;
}

static PyObject *myFunc(MyObject *self, PyObject *args)
{
  printf("%d\n", self->myVal);
  printf("hello world\n");
  Py_RETURN_NONE;
};

static PyMemberDef myMemberdef[] = {
    {"MyVar", T_INT, offsetof(MyObject, myVal), 0,
                                    "MyInstanceAttr"},
    {"MyAttr", T_OBJECT_EX, offsetof(MyObject, myAttr), 0,
                                    "MyInstandeAttr"},
    {NULL}};

static PyMethodDef myMethodDef[] = {
    {"MyMethod", (PyCFunction)myFunc, METH_VARARGS,
                                    "the doc string"},
    {NULL}};

static PyTypeObject MyType1 = {
    .ob_base = PyVarObject_HEAD_INIT(NULL, 0)
    .tp_name = "example.myObject",
    .tp_doc = PyDoc_STR("My Custom object"),
    .tp_flags = Py_TPFLAGS_DEFAULT | Py_TPFLAGS_HAVE_GC,
    .tp_basicsize = sizeof(MyObject),
    .tp_itemsize = 0,
    .tp_new = PyType_GenericNew,
    .tp_init = (initproc)Custom_init,
    .tp_members = myMemberdef,
    .tp_methods = myMethodDef,
    .tp_clear = (inquiry)Custom_clear,
    .tp_traverse = (traverseproc)Custom_traverse,
    .tp_dealloc = (destructor)Custom_dealloc,
};

static struct PyModuleDef myModule = {
    PyModuleDef_HEAD_INIT,
    "example",
    "C library to test API",
    -1,
    NULL};
```

```
PyMODINIT_FUNC PyInit_example(void)
{
  PyObject *m = PyModule_Create(&myModule);
  if (m == NULL)
    return NULL;
  int res = PyType_Ready(&MyType1);
  PyModule_AddObject(m, "MyClass", (PyObject *)&MyType1);
  return m;
}
```

Notice that we can rely on the GenericNew function to use the correct memory allocator and so we don't need a custom new function but a custom init function has been defined. Notice that while None cannot be deallocated, you do have to keep its reference count accurate.

If you try this out:

```
import example
import gc

myInst1=example.MyClass()
print(gc.is_tracked(myInst1))
myInst1.MyAttr=myInst1
myInst1=None
print(gc.get_count())
gc.collect()
print(gc.get_count())
```

You will see that the destructor is now called when you force a garbage collection. In other words, the self-reference loop is detected and the instance is removed correctly. You can also see that calling the GC using collect reduces the number of objects waiting for collection to zero. You will also notice that the traverse function is called a number of times as the GC analyses the references. The clear function is called twice – once by the GC to clear all objects references and once by the destructor itself before it deallocates the object. You might think that you can remove the call to clear from the destructor, but if you do this the references will not decremented when the destructor is called due to a simple zero reference count. As the clear function can handle attributes that have already been set to NULL, there is no problem in calling it twice.

tp_dealloc and tp_finalize

Most of the current code in the Python system implements the destructor as described above, using `tp_dealloc` for both simple zero reference count and cycle breaking deallocation. However, there are warnings that the destructor might trigger another round of garbage collection and this could leave the original object in an unstable state:

> *"There are limitations to what you can safely do in a deallocator function. First, if your type supports garbage collection (using `tp_traverse` and/or `tp_clear`), some of the object's members can have been cleared or finalized by the time `tp_dealloc` is called. Second, in `tp_dealloc`, your object is in an unstable state: its reference count is equal to zero. Any call to a non-trivial object or API might end up calling `tp_dealloc` again, causing a double free and a crash.*
>
> *Starting with Python 3.4, it is recommended not to put any complex finalization code in `tp_dealloc`, and instead use the new `tp_finalize` type method."*

The situation is confused and the documentation doesn't make it clear how to proceed. It helps to distinguish two situations in which an object needs to be deallocated – when its reference count is reduced to zero and when it is part of an isolated cycle.

The destructor referenced by `tp_dealloc` is called in both situations, but there are rare cases when it will fail in the isolated cycle case because the deallocation of the object triggers other deallocations which leave it in an unstable state. Currently most Python code uses this approach.

If you define `tp_finalize` and not `tp_dealloc` then the destructor is only called when an isolated cycle is being deallocated. That is, the function referenced by `tp_finalize` is not called for objects that simply have a zero reference count – this will result in a memory leak.

If you define both then everything works for a simple zero reference count as `tp_finalize` isn't called in this case, but for the deallocation of an isolated cycle both are called, first `tp_finalize` which deallocates the object and then `tp_dealloc` which fails because the object has already been deallocated.

There is no approved way of handling this situation, but the following works. If you define a different function for `tp_dealloc` and `tp_finalize` you can code the first to clean up objects with zero references and the second to clean up an isolated cycle. To stop the `tp_dealloc` function trying to deallocate an object that has already been deallocated you have to use the `PyObject_GC_IsFinalized` function to test that the object hasn't already been removed. For example, we can convert the previous example to use tp_finalize and tp_dealloc. The modifications required are:

```
static void Custom_finalizer(MyObject *self)
{
  printf("finalizer called\n");
  if (PyObject_GC_IsFinalized((PyObject *)self))
    return;
  PyObject *error_type, *error_value, *error_traceback;
  PyErr_Fetch(&error_type, &error_value, &error_traceback);
  PyObject_GC_UnTrack(self);
  Py_TYPE(self)->tp_clear((PyObject *)self);
  PyObject_GC_Del(self);
  PyErr_Restore(error_type, error_value, error_traceback);
}
```

and:

```
static PyTypeObject MyType1 = {
    .ob_base = PyVarObject_HEAD_INIT(NULL, 0)
                 .tp_name = "example.myObject",
. . .
    .tp_clear = (inquiry)Custom_clear,
    .tp_traverse = (traverseproc)Custom_traverse,
    .tp_finalize = (destructor)Custom_finalizer,
    .tp_dealloc = (destructor)Custom_dealloc,
};
```

With these changes the program runs correctly and deallocates objects irrespective of whether they are subject to a zero reference count or an isolated loop. It also has the side effect of avoiding calling tp_clear twice.

A full listing can be found on the book's webpage.

Dynamic Types

So far all the type objects we have created have been static. The instances they create have been dynamic in the sense that they are created on the heap. To get the full behavior of a Python class as an extension you need to create the type object on the heap, i.e. a dynamic type. A dynamic type is mutable and it can engage in multiple inheritance whereas a static type is immutable and can only engage in single inheritance.

From the point of the rest of the API, heap-allocated types aren't that different from static types – just an area of memory with a particular interpretation. What differs is in how you create a heap type and, more precisely, how you set its slots. A static type can have its slots initialized at load time, but a heap type has to have its slots initialized when it is created, i.e. at run time. The solution to this is to have a function which creates the struct on the heap and then initializes it according the values in a standard static struct.

The functions which create the type object are:

- PyObject *PyType_FromModuleAndSpec(PyObject *module,
                                  PyType_Spec *spec, PyObject *bases)
- PyObject *PyType_FromSpecWithBases(PyType_Spec *spec,
                                  PyObject *bases)
- PyObject *PyType_FromSpec(PyType_Spec *spec)

The first allows you to specify the spec, module and bases to use for inheritance, the second just the bases and the final just the spec. Notice that bases is a tuple of base types or a single base class. The function allocates the memory indeed for the struct and initialize it, sets Py_TPFLAGS_HEAPTYPE flag and calls PyType_Ready(). You don't have to supply a tp_new or a tp_init and you can ignore the header macros as the functions construct the type struct with them automatically included.

The spec is a struct that specifies the most important slots:

```
typedef struct{
    const char* name;
    int basicsize;
    int itemsize;
    unsigned int flags;
    PyType_Slot *slots; /* terminated by slot==0. */
} PyType_Spec;
```

The fields are the same as in the static type struct. The final field is an array of another struct that lets you set optional slots. Each slot element is:

```
typedef struct{
    int slot;    /* slot id */
    void *pfunc; /* function pointer */
} PyType_Slot;
```

The slot id can be specified using defined constants with the same name as the slot with Py_ prefixed. For example, if you want to set tp_doc you would use:

```
{Py_tp_doc, "My Custom object"},
```

You only have to set the slots you want to make use of.

A simple example is to convert the type object we used earlier with a single int attribute and a simple method:

```c
#define PY_SSIZE_T_CLEAN
#include <Python.h>
#include <stddef.h>
#include "structmember.h"
typedef struct
{
    PyObject_HEAD
    int myVal;
} MyObject;
static PyObject *myFunc(MyObject *self, PyObject *args)
{
    printf("%d\n", self->myVal);
    printf("hello world\n");
    Py_RETURN_NONE;
};
static PyMemberDef myMemberdef[] = {
    {"MyVar", T_INT, offsetof(MyObject, myVal), 0,
                                    "MyInstanceAttr"},
    {NULL}};
static PyMethodDef myMethodDef[] = {
    {"MyMethod", (PyCFunction)myFunc, METH_VARARGS,
                                    "the doc string"},
    {NULL}};
static struct PyModuleDef myModule = {PyModuleDef_HEAD_INIT,
            "example", "C library to test API", -1, NULL};

PyMODINIT_FUNC PyInit_example(void)
{
    PyObject *m = PyModule_Create(&myModule);
    if (m == NULL)
        return NULL;
    static PyType_Slot mySlots[] = {
        {Py_tp_doc, "My Custom object"},
        {Py_tp_members, myMemberdef},
        {Py_tp_methods, myMethodDef},
        {0, NULL}};
    PyType_Spec mySpec = {
        "example.myObject",
        sizeof(MyObject),
        0,
        Py_TPFLAGS_DEFAULT,
        mySlots};
    PyTypeObject *MyType1 = (PyTypeObject *)
                                    PyType_FromSpec(&mySpec);
    PyModule_AddObject(m, "MyClass", (PyObject *)MyType1);
    return m;
}
```

If you run this you will find that MyClass has attribute MyVar and you can write things like:

```
import example
myInst1 = example.MyClass()
myInst1.MyVar = 42
print(myInst1.MyVar)
myInst1.MyMethod()
```

which is exactly what you could have done with the static version. What you couldn't have done is:

```
example.MyClass.myNewVar = 43
print(example.MyClass.myNewVar)
```

This works and you will see 43 displayed as the value of the new attribute. This neatly demonstrates that the static type is immutable the heap type is mutable.

Heap Types With GC

In general, heap types should support full GC. You can usually just convert a static type into a heap type by editing the type struct into a suitable spec and using this in PyType_FromSpec. For example, to convert the full GC example to a heap type all we need to do is change the way the slots are specified:

```
static PyType_Slot mySlots[] = {
    {Py_tp_doc, "My Custom object"},
    {Py_tp_members, myMemberdef},
    {Py_tp_methods, myMethodDef},
    {Py_tp_clear, (inquiry)Custom_clear},
    {Py_tp_traverse, (traverseproc)Custom_traverse},
    {Py_tp_dealloc, (destructor)Custom_dealloc},
    {Py_tp_finalize,(destructor)Custom_finalizer},
    {0, NULL}};

  PyType_Spec mySpec = {
      "example.myObject",
      sizeof(MyObject),
      0,
      Py_TPFLAGS_DEFAULT| Py_TPFLAGS_HAVE_GC,
      mySlots};

PyMODINIT_FUNC PyInit_example(void)
{
  PyObject *m = PyModule_Create(&myModule);
  if (m == NULL)
    return NULL;
  PyTypeObject *MyType1 = (PyTypeObject *)PyType_FromSpec(&mySpec);
  PyModule_AddObject(m, "MyClass", (PyObject *)MyType1);
  return m;
}
```

With this change the class behaves in the same way as the static version and the destructor is called when a reference loop is detected as before.

The full program listing can be found on the book's webpage.

Inheritance

If you set the `tp_base` slot or the `bases` parameter for a heap type then you can specify some other types to act as the base classes. Recall that static types can only inherit from a single base class. Generally this isn't a limiting factor so we can begin by looking at inheritance in the static case.

The mechanism of inheritance in Python is very simple. The base class simply puts its struct at the start of the derived class's struct for the instance. So if `MyObject` is inheriting from `MyBase` the struct for the instance is:

```
typedef struct
{
  MyBaseObject super;
  int myVal;
  PyObject *myAttr;
  other MyObject specific fields
} MyObject;
```

This allows the struct to be cast as a `MyBase*` or `MyObject*` or, of course, `PyObject`. You can see that an instance has all of the fields of `MyBase` and the fields specific to `MyObject`.

In addition the `MyObjectType` object has a reference to the `MyBaseType` object as its `tp_base` slot. Some slots are inherited and others aren't – you need to consult the documentation to find out which. The inherited slots are copied when you call `PyType_Ready` and they provide the inherited behavior of the derived type along with the struct that provides the instance. In most cases you can assume that the base type's `new` and `init` will be called automatically and this will construct the combined `MyObject` struct. You may have to call a custom `init` to initialize the new part of the struct and if this is the case you have to arrange to explicitly call the base type's `init`.

A simple example will make the basic ideas clearer. We can add the Python `str` type as a base class to our simple example given earlier, but without any garbage collection to keep the example simple.

First we need to extend the `struct` used for the instance:

```
typedef struct
{
  PyUnicodeObject str;
  int myVal;
  PyObject *myAttr;
} MyObject;
```

Notice that we are using `PyUnicodeObject` not the related type object, i.e. the struct that gives the instance rather than the class. All Python objects have a type object and an instance struct which defines the fields in the block of memory allocated to the instance.

All we have to do is set up the custom type:

```
static PyTypeObject MyType1 = {
    .ob_base = PyVarObject_HEAD_INIT(NULL, 0)
    .tp_name = "example.myObject",
    .tp_doc = PyDoc_STR("My Custom object"),
    .tp_flags = Py_TPFLAGS_DEFAULT | Py_TPFLAGS_BASETYPE,
    .tp_basicsize = sizeof(MyObject),
    .tp_itemsize = 0,
    .tp_members = myMemberdef,
    .tp_methods = myMethodDef,
};
```

Notice that we don't need to specify a `tp_new` or a `tp_init` these are supplied by inheritance from the base class. We do need to set the `tp_flags` to indicate that we are using a base class. The only other change we need to make is to set `tp_base` in the module initialization function:

```
PyMODINIT_FUNC PyInit_example(void)
{
  PyObject *m = PyModule_Create(&myModule);
  if (m == NULL)
    return NULL;
  MyType1.tp_base = &PyUnicode_Type;
  int res = PyType_Ready(&MyType1);
  PyModule_AddObject(m, "MyClass", (PyObject *)&MyType1);
  return m;
}
```

You have to do it this way as some systems will display a compiler error if you try to set it as part of the `struct` initialization. Notice that we have to set `tp_base` to the type object's struct.

The complete listing is:

```c
#define PY_SSIZE_T_CLEAN
#include <Python.h>
#include <stddef.h>
#include "structmember.h"

typedef struct
{
  PyUnicodeObject str;
  int myVal;
  PyObject *myAttr;
} MyObject;

static PyObject *myFunc(MyObject *self, PyObject *args)
{
  printf("%d\n", self->myVal);
  printf("hello world\n");
  Py_RETURN_NONE;
};

static PyMemberDef myMemberdef[] = {
    {"MyVar", T_INT, offsetof(MyObject, myVal), 0,
                                        "MyInstanceAttr"},
    {"MyAttr", T_OBJECT_EX, offsetof(MyObject, myAttr), 0,
                                        "MyInstandeAttr"},
    {NULL}};

static PyMethodDef myMethodDef[] = {
    {"MyMethod", (PyCFunction)myFunc, METH_VARARGS,
                                        "the doc string"},
    {NULL}};

static PyTypeObject MyType1 = {
    .ob_base = PyVarObject_HEAD_INIT(NULL, 0)
    .tp_name = "example.myObject",
    .tp_doc = PyDoc_STR("My Custom object"),
    .tp_flags = Py_TPFLAGS_DEFAULT | Py_TPFLAGS_BASETYPE,
    .tp_basicsize = sizeof(MyObject),
    .tp_itemsize = 0,
    .tp_members = myMemberdef,
    .tp_methods = myMethodDef,
};

static struct PyModuleDef myModule = {
    PyModuleDef_HEAD_INIT,
    "example",
    "C library to test API",
    -1,
    NULL};
```

```
PyMODINIT_FUNC PyInit_example(void)
{
  PyObject *m = PyModule_Create(&myModule);
  if (m == NULL)
    return NULL;
  MyType1.tp_base = &PyUnicode_Type;
  int res = PyType_Ready(&MyType1);
  PyModule_AddObject(m, "MyClass", (PyObject *)&MyType1);
  return m;
}
```

If you try this out you will find we have a `str` object which also has a `MyVar` and a `MyAttr` attribute and a `MyMethod` method:

```
import example
myInst1 = example.MyClass("Hello")
print(len(myInst1))
myInst1.MyVar = 42
print(myInst1.MyVar)
myInst1.MyMethod()
print("myInst=",myInst1)
```

When you print `len` and `myInst1` you can see that it really does behave like a `str` object, but it also has additional attributes and methods. If you start to examine what we have created you might be less impressed by its usefulness. In particular, if you use any of the string methods on `myInst` you will discover that things go wrong:

```
result = myInst1.upper()
print(result)
result.MyVar = 43
```

The upper method returns a new `str` object and while this does have the same content as `myInst1` it is a `str` object and not a `MyClass2` object and it has none of the additional attributes – you get an error message on the last instruction stating that result doesn't have a `MyVar` attribute. We may have succeeded in subclassing `str`, but we haven't changed the way string methods work and this is a standard problem with subclasing any immutable object – the methods don't change the original object, but create a new instance of the base class.

Subclassing – init and GC

In general it is more useful to subclass mutable objects.

We need to override slots and their associated functions in the derived class. For example, we need a custom init to set `MyVar` to something before the instance is used. Immutable classes such as `str` generally don't implement an init and they don't engage in garbage collection beyond simple reference counting. The list type makes a better example of implementing both of these aspects of inheritance.

To inherit from list all we have to do is change the previous example to use PyListObject and PyList_Type instead of the Unicode string object and type:

```
typedef struct
{
  PyListObject list;
  int myVal;
  PyObject *myAttr;
} MyObject;


PyMODINIT_FUNC PyInit_example(void)
{
  PyObject *m = PyModule_Create(&myModule);
  if (m == NULL)
    return NULL;

  MyType1.tp_base = &PyList_Type;
  int res = PyType_Ready(&MyType1);
  PyModule_AddObject(m, "MyClass", (PyObject *)&MyType1);
  return m;
}
```

With these changes you can write Python programs like:

```
import example
myInst1 = example.MyClass(["brian","spam",42])
print(myInst1)
print(len(myInst1))
```

and you will see ['brian', 'spam', 42], 3 displayed. MyClass is effectively a list.

If we now define a custom init we will have to call the base class init - at the moment it is called by inheritance;

```
static int Custom_init(MyObject *self, PyObject *args,
                                       PyObject *kwds)
{
  int res=Py_TYPE(self)->tp_base-> tp_init((PyObject *)self,
                                           args, kwds);
  self->myVal= PyList_Size((PyObject*) self);
  return 0;
}
```

Notice that we have to call the base init before working with the object for obvious reasons.

The custom init and methods in general can use C API functions to work with the base class attributes. In this case we use PyList_Size to store the size, i.e. the number of elements in an instance variable. We also need to add this to the type:

```
static PyTypeObject MyType1 = {
    .ob_base = PyVarObject_HEAD_INIT(NULL, 0)
    .tp_name = "example.myObject",
    .tp_doc = PyDoc_STR("My Custom object"),
    .tp_flags = Py_TPFLAGS_DEFAULT | Py_TPFLAGS_BASETYPE,
    .tp_basicsize = sizeof(MyObject),
    .tp_itemsize = 0,
    .tp_init = (initproc)Custom_init,
    .tp_members = myMemberdef,
    .tp_methods = myMethodDef,
};
```

With these changes we can write Python programs like:

```
myInst1=example.MyClass2(["brian","spam",42])
print(myInst1)
print(len(myInst1))
print(myInst1.MyVar)
```

and you will see that MyVar agrees with len(myInst1).

In general, call the base class init function before performing any initalizations specific to the derived class.

Next we have to deal with the problem of garbage collection. In this case we have to use the base class to do most of the work – after all it knows how to deallocate itself. The only additional work that the derived class has to do is to dereference anything that it has added to the base class. There is the added problem of how to handle tp_dealloc and tp_finalize, but in practice you can simply call the base class's tp_dealloc and put up with the unlikely event that an object being deallocated is in an unstable state.

The destructor needed is:

```
static void Custom_dealloc(MyObject *self)
{
  PyObject *error_type,*error_value, *error_traceback;
  PyErr_Fetch(&error_type, &error_value, &error_traceback);
  Py_TYPE(self)->tp_clear((PyObject *)self);
  Py_TYPE(self)->tp_base->tp_dealloc((PyObject *)self);
  PyErr_Restore(error_type, error_value, error_traceback);
}
```

Notice that there is no need to call PyObject_GC_UnTrack or PyObject_GC_Del as the inherited destructor calls both. If the base class doesn't then some class on the inheritance chain will.

The `clear` function should decrement the reference count of any Python fields that the derived class has added. In this case:

```c
static int Custom_clear(MyObject *self)
{
  printf("clear called\n");
  Py_CLEAR(self->myAttr);
  return 0;
}
```

Notice that we call `tp_clear` before calling the base destructor. In general you can ignore defining `tp_finalize` as most built-in classes don't use it.

Finally we need to call the base class traverse function in the `custom_traverse` – if we didn't then isolated reference loops in its fields would not be detected:

```c
static int Custom_traverse(MyObject *self, visitproc visit,
                                                void *arg)
{
  printf("traverse called\n");
  Py_VISIT(self->myAttr);
  PyList_Type.tp_traverse((PyObject *)self,visit,arg);
  return 0;
}
```

The complete listing is:

```c
#define PY_SSIZE_T_CLEAN
#include <Python.h>
#include <stddef.h>
#include "structmember.h"
typedef struct
{
  PyListObject list;
  int myVal;
  PyObject *myAttr;
} MyObject;

static PyObject *myFunc(MyObject *self, PyObject *args)
{
  printf("%d\n", self->myVal);
  printf("hello world\n");
  Py_RETURN_NONE;
};

static int Custom_init(MyObject *self, PyObject *args,
                                                PyObject *kwds)
{
  int res = Py_TYPE(self)->tp_base->tp_init((PyObject *)self,
                                                args, kwds);
  self->myVal = PyList_Size((PyObject *)self);
  return 0;
}
```

```c
static void Custom_dealloc(MyObject *self)
{
  printf("destructor called\n");
  PyObject *error_type, *error_value, *error_traceback;
  PyErr_Fetch(&error_type, &error_value, &error_traceback);
  Py_TYPE(self)->tp_clear((PyObject *)self);
  Py_TYPE(self)->tp_base->tp_dealloc((PyObject *)self);
  PyErr_Restore(error_type, error_value, error_traceback);
}

static int Custom_clear(MyObject *self)
{
  printf("clear called\n");
  Py_CLEAR(self->myAttr);
  return 0;
}

static int Custom_traverse(MyObject *self, visitproc visit,
                                            void *arg)
{
  printf("traverse called\n");
  Py_VISIT(self->myAttr);
  PyList_Type.tp_traverse((PyObject *)self, visit, arg);
  return 0;
}

static PyMemberDef myMemberdef[] = {
    {"MyVar", T_INT, offsetof(MyObject, myVal), 0,
                                    "MyInstanceAttr"},
    {"MyAttr", T_OBJECT_EX, offsetof(MyObject, myAttr), 0,
                                    "MyInstandeAttr"},
    {NULL}};

static PyMethodDef myMethodDef[] = {
    {"MyMethod", (PyCFunction)myFunc, METH_VARARGS,
                                    "the doc string"},
    {NULL}};

static PyTypeObject MyType1 = {
    .ob_base = PyVarObject_HEAD_INIT(NULL, 0)
    .tp_name = "example.myObject",
    .tp_doc = PyDoc_STR("My Custom object"),
    .tp_flags = Py_TPFLAGS_DEFAULT | Py_TPFLAGS_BASETYPE,
    .tp_basicsize = sizeof(MyObject),
    .tp_itemsize = 0,
    .tp_members = myMemberdef,
    .tp_methods = myMethodDef,
    .tp_init = (initproc)Custom_init,
    .tp_clear = (inquiry)Custom_clear,
    .tp_traverse = (traverseproc)Custom_traverse,
    .tp_dealloc = (destructor)Custom_dealloc,
};
```

```
static struct PyModuleDef myModule = {
    PyModuleDef_HEAD_INIT,
    "example",
    "C library to test API",
    -1,
    NULL};

PyMODINIT_FUNC PyInit_example(void)
{
  PyObject *m = PyModule_Create(&myModule);
  if (m == NULL)
    return NULL;

  MyType1.tp_base = &PyList_Type;
  int res = PyType_Ready(&MyType1);
  PyModule_AddObject(m, "MyClass", (PyObject *)&MyType1);
  return m;
}
```

Object Factories

An object factory is simply a function that returns an instance of a class, i.e. an object. In this sense the class itself is the archetypal object factory. There are lots of times, however, when the simplest option is to create a custom object factory and bypass the use of the class.

We need to create an instance of the class. The most obvious way to do this is to call the type's new function followed by the init function, however this is unnecessarily complicated. The type is itself a callable and when called it is the same as calling the constructor. Calling the constructor is converted into a call to the type object in pure Python programs.

To create a callable all you have to do is specify the function you want to call in the tp_call slot. The function has to have the signature:

```
PyObject *tp_call(PyObject *callable, PyObject *args,
                                      PyObject *kwargs)
```

To call a Python function or a callable from C we need to use:

- ◆ `PyObject *PyObject_Call(PyObject *callable, PyObject *args,`
  `                                        PyObject *kwargs)`

There are a set of Call functions which are used to call different types of Python function. The simple Call presents the args as a tuple and kwargs as a dict or NULL.

The type object is a callable so we can get an instance of the type by calling it and create a factory function by returning the result:

```
static PyObject *myFactory(PyObject *self, PyObject *args)
{
  args = Py_BuildValue("()");
  PyObject *result = PyObject_Call((PyObject *)self, args, NULL);
  return result;
}
```

We can arrange for self to be set to MyType1 when we convert the C function to a Python function using PyCFunction_New.

This can be added to the module:

```
static PyMethodDef myFactory_def = {
    "myFactory",
    (PyCFunction)myFactory,
    METH_FASTCALL | METH_KEYWORDS,
    "the doc string"};

PyMODINIT_FUNC PyInit_example(void)
{
  PyObject *m = PyModule_Create(&myModule);
  if (m == NULL)
    return NULL;

  PyObject *myPyFactory = PyCFunction_New(&myFactory_def,
                                          (PyObject*) &MyType1);
  PyModule_AddObject(m, "myFactory", myPyFactory);

  int res = PyType_Ready(&MyType1);
  PyModule_AddObject(m, "MyClass", (PyObject *)&MyType1);

  return m;
}
```

With this defined we can write programs like:

```
import example
myInst=example.myFactory()
print(myInst)
print(myInst.MyVar)
myInst.MyVar=42
print(myInst.MyVar)
```

The full program is on the book's webpage. You can also disable the ability to use the constructor to create an instance.

Calling Python

You can also use the call function to call existing Python functions. For example:

```
static PyObject *call(PyObject *self, PyObject *args)
{
  PyObject *math = PyImport_AddModule("math");
  PyObject *mathdict = PyModule_GetDict(math);
  PyObject *myFunction = PyDict_GetItemString(mathdict, "sqrt");
  args = Py_BuildValue("(I)", 2);
  PyObject *result = PyObject_Call(myFunction, args, NULL);
  return result;
}
```

This gets a reference to the math module and then uses its dict to get a reference to the sqrt function and finally calls it.

Using a similar technique you can also create an instance of a class defined in the main program:

```
static PyObject *object1(PyObject *self, PyObject *args)
{
  PyObject *main = PyImport_AddModule("__main__");
  PyObject *maindict = PyModule_GetDict(main);
  PyObject *myclass = PyDict_GetItemString(maindict, "myClass");
  args = Py_BuildValue("()");
  PyObject *result = PyObject_Call(myclass, args, NULL);
  PyObject *newValue = PyLong_FromLong(43);
  PyObject_SetAttrString(result, "myAttribute1", newValue);
  return result;
}
```

This assumes that the main program contains a class called myClass with an attribute called myAttribute. The function creates an instance, changes the value of myAttribute and then return the instance. For example:

```
import example
import math
class myClass:
 myAttribute1=0

print(example.call())

inst=example.object1()
print(inst)
print(inst.myAttribute1)
```

displays

```
1.4142135623730951
<__main__.myClass object at 0xf70b4d50>
43
```

There are a great many variations on this sort of use of existing Python functions and classes, but they make use of the same basic functions to import or add modules, get the module dict and use it to find the object you want to use and then call and access its attributes.

The full program is on the book's webpage.

Summary

- Python's reference counting garbage collection involves defining a destructor function to clean up any resources that an object has created.

- As well as reference counting garbage collection, we also need to deal with reference cycles that could result in an inaccessible object having a non-zero reference count.

- You can avoid some cyclic references by using a weak reference.

- The complete solution to cyclic references is to support the full Python garbage collector. To do this you need to set the object to be tracked and define a function to determine which attributes are to be tracked. You need a function to clear attribute references in addition to the destructor function.

- The `tp_finalize` slot was introduced to improve on `tp_dealloc`, but it is best used to handle cyclic reference deallocation.

- Dynamic types are allocated on the heap. Apart from having to use a function to initialize the slots, they works in much the same way.

- Inheritance is implemented by setting the `tp_base` slot or the `bases` parameter for a heap type and using the base class object struct as the start of the derived class struct.

- If you define a custom `init` in the derived class you should call the base class `init` before doing anything else.

- Derived classes should clean up their own resources before calling the base class `tp_decalloc` and use the base class `clean` and `traverse` to ensure that the inherited resources are garbage-collected.

- A type is callable and this can be used to construct an instance, making implementing object factories easy.

- You can use the same callable mechanism to call Python constructors from C.

Chapter 14

Threads And The GIL

Most Python programmers have heard about the GIL – Global Interpreter Lock. This is the mechanism that ensures that at any given time only a single thread is using the Python system. Most Python programmers can ignore the GIL and accept it as a way of making sure that their programs run securely even if they make use of C extensions that are multithreaded. The cost of this security is that they cannot make use of multiple cores that their machine might offer to speed up their programs.

In this chapter we take a look at the effect of the GIL on C extensions. Even if you are writing a simple extension function and have no intention of using multiple threads, your creation can still be impacted by the GIL. It is assumed that you know something about async programming in both Python and C. In the case of C, although the details of threading vary according to the operating system, Windows threading and Linux Pthreads are very similar in operation. The examples that follow present both approaches but you are expected to already know something about threading in the relevant OS. If you need a refresher for Linux see Chapter 12, Threads, of *Applying C For The IoT With Linux*, ISBN: 978-1871962611, which can be found as an extract on the I Programmer website, www.i-programmer.info.

At the time of writing there are plans to deprecate the GIL. However, even if it is removed by default there will be a large number of users who opt to run Python with it enabled and this means that extension writers cannot ignore it. As an intermediate solution Python is also in the process of acquiring the ability to run multiple copies of the interpreter – sub-interpreters – each one capable of running on a separate core. This is likely to be an important way of improving Python performance in the future and we have already covered some of the techniques needed to make use of it, in particular multi-phase initialization of modules. In most case it is going to be more efficient to develop an extension without supporting sub-interpreters and adding this feature later.

How Threads Interact With The GIL

The Python system is not designed to be shared by multiple threads of execution – it is not "thread-safe". Threads are very different from processes in that they share the runtime environment. That is, they have access to the same set of variables and objects as they run within the same process. Processes, on the other hand, each have their own copies of all of the variables within the program and there is no interaction between them. This sharing of resources seems to make things simpler, but in many ways it creates additional problems.

At the time of writing another major issue is the GIL – Global Interpreter Lock. The current implementation of CPython, and some other implementations like PyPy, allow only one thread to use the Python interpreter code at any one time. This isn't very important on a system that has only a single CPU or core as only one thread is active at any given time anyway, but it does stop programs from running faster on multicore machines.

The main reasons for the continued existence of the GIL are that it allows Python to work with C-based libraries that are not thread-safe and to ensure the single-threaded programs, which account for most Python programs are fast.

To be clear there are two types of thread involved – Python threads and C threads. Python threads are created by the Python program and they run code using the Python interpreter. They are essentially C threads with some extra data and Python methods to wrap them. In this case the GIL blocks all but one Python thread from running at a time. If a Python program calls a Python function implemented as a C program then it is possible that it runs for some of the time not accessing any Python resources. In this case it is usual for the C program to release the GIL. Of course, this has no effect if the Python program is single-threaded as there is no other thread to take advantage of the situation. Things only get interesting if there are other threads, be they Python threads or C threads.

A Python thread also gives up the GIL every so often to give other threads a chance to run. This aspect of the GIL was changed in Python 3.9 to make it work better. Originally a thread holding the GIL was allowed to execute a fixed number of Python byte codes. Now it runs for a maximum time before relinquishing the GIL and allowing another thread to run. The operating system decides which of the waiting threads gets to run.

You can find out what this time interval is and set it using:

```
sys.getswitchinterval()
sys.setswitchinterval(value)
```

Currently the default is 0.005 s, i.e. 5 ms. Given that switching threads is an expensive operation the value should be set high, but you can improve the response time of a program by lowering it. Notice that the system may not set the exact value you specify – it could be longer. Also the default of 5 ms is very long by comparison with the execution times of many threads and so it is often possible for a thread to run to completion without being interrupted by another thread.

When an extension is called, it is always called using a thread that has the GIL, which means that the extension can make use of the entire Python API without having to worry that some other thread will cause a problem.

To summarize:

- Only one thread has the GIL and hence is running Python code at any given time, no matter how many cores the machine has.

- A thread that starts to execute non-Python code, usually C code, should give up the GIL and allow another thread to run Python code.

- A thread should give up the GIL and allows another thread to run if it starts an I/O or other operation that causes it to have to wait.

- A thread also gives up the GIL after `switchinterval` seconds and allows another thread to acquire the GIL and run.

- Any extension code is always run using a thread the has the GIL and this means it can be sure that no other thread will modify anything it is working with.

The GIL is a confusing factor when you are trying to reason about the behavior of a threaded program. Things don't always work as you would expect from a consideration of the way the operating system handles threading. In this sense the GIL gets in the way of the OS scheduler and stops it from doing its job.

C Functions On A Python Thread

There is a tendency to think that if you are writing an extension function or class that doesn't use threading you can ignore problems with the GIL. This isn't necessarily the case - you might not use threads but another Python programmer using your extension might not agree and might deploy it in one or more threads. For example, consider the `Pi` function given in Chapter 4 which has been constructed with no thought of the GIL:

```c
#define PY_SSIZE_T_CLEAN
#include <Python.h>
#if defined(_WIN32) || defined(_WIN64)
#define SCALE 1000
#else
#define SCALE 1
#endif

static PyObject *Pi(PyObject *self, PyObject *args)
{
    int m, n;
    double pi, s;
    if (!PyArg_ParseTuple(args, "ii", &m, &n))
        return NULL;
    pi = 0;
    for (int k = m; k < n; k++)
    {
        s = 1;
        if (k % 2 == 0)
            s = -1;
        pi = pi + s / (2 * k - 1);
    }
    sleep(5 * SCALE);
    return PyFloat_FromDouble(4 * pi);
}
static PyMethodDef AddMethods[] = {
    {"myPi", (PyCFunction)Pi, METH_VARARGS, "Compute Pi"},
    {NULL, NULL, 0, NULL} // sentinel
};
static struct PyModuleDef addmodule = {
    PyModuleDef_HEAD_INIT,
    "Pi",
    "C library to compute Pi",
    -1,
    AddMethods};

PyMODINIT_FUNC PyInit_Pi(void)
{
    return PyModule_Create(&addmodule);
}
```

The only change here to the previous Pi function is the inclusion of a `Sleep` call so as to slow things down so that we can see what is happening when the function is called on a new thread. Notice that Linux implements `Sleep` using seconds and Windows uses milliseconds, hence the need to modify the argument after detecting the OS.

With this extension a Python programmer could write:

```python
import Pi
import time
import concurrent.futures
N=10000000
with concurrent.futures.ThreadPoolExecutor() as executor:
    t1=time.perf_counter()
    f1 = executor.submit(Pi.myPi,1,N)
    t2=time.perf_counter()
    print("do some additional work")
    print("waiting for result")
    print(f1.result())
    print((t2-t1)*1000)
```

The `ThreadPoolExecutor` allows you to start a function on a new thread and:

```python
 f1 = executor.submit(Pi.myPi,1,N)
```

runs myPi(1,N) on a new thread and you would expect it to return immediately with a future. Or rather this is what is supposed to happen. You can then do other tasks and check that the function has completed by calling the future's result method. If you want to know more about promises/futures and executors see *Programmer's Python: Async* ISBN: 978-1871962595.

However, things don't work out as expected. Notice that the Python programmer has called your extension function using a separate thread without you having to make any modifications or allowances in your code. The new thread that the Pi function is run on has the GIL and this means that the main thread cannot proceed to run Python. The Pi function retains ownership of the GIL until it ends and only then can the main thread acquire the GIL and continue. Thus the call to `executor.submit` doesn't return immediately with a promise – it acts as a blocking call, even though it is running on a different thread, because it owns the GIL. If you run this program you will see the messages only after 5s has passed:

```
do some additional work
waiting for result
3.1415927535898014
5052.7309000026435
```

The solution to the problem is to release the GIL and this can be done by adding just two lines to the function.

The:

`Py_BEGIN_ALLOW_THREADS`

macro opens a new block and saves the status of the thread in a hidden variable before releasing the GIL. This has to be followed by:

`Py_END_ALLOW_THREADS`

which restores the status, acquires the GIL and ends the block. Notice that the thread in question is a Python thread and so it has status information.

Also notice that the two macros form a block and so any variables declared within the block are local to the block. There is also the possibility that the thread has to wait for the GIL to become free and this could slow things down. In this case there is no detectable difference in the time it takes to compute Pi when the `Sleep` is removed.

If the `Pi` function is changed to read:

```c
static PyObject *Pi(PyObject *self, PyObject *args)
{
    int m, n;
    double pi, s;

    if (!PyArg_ParseTuple(args, "ii", &m, &n))
        return NULL;
    Py_BEGIN_ALLOW_THREADS
    pi = 0;
    for (int k = m; k < n; k++)
    {
        s = 1;
        if (k % 2 == 0)
            s = -1;
        pi = pi + s / (2 * k - 1);
    }
    sleep(5 * SCALE);
    Py_END_ALLOW_THREADS
    return PyFloat_FromDouble(4 * pi);
}
```

and the Python program is run again the promise is returned immediately and the message

```
do some additional work
waiting for result
```

appears almost at once and then five seconds later you will see:

```
3.1415927535898014
5052.7309000026435
```

With the release of the GIL the program works as the Python programmer would expect.

This idea generalizes and you should release the GIL whenever you are not using the Python API for any significant length of time – a long computation or waiting for I/O, for example. Do not release the GIL if you are going to need to acquire it a few instructions later as this will slow your extension down.

Non-Python Threads

As well as your C code being run on a Python thread, there is nothing stopping you from creating raw C threads to speed up your extension or to keep it active. Non-Python threads do not interact with the GIL. The main thread which has the GIL when your extension is called can release it or keep it with no effect on any raw threads you might have created. Of course, a raw Python thread should not access the C API without acquiring the GIL and to do this it has to be converted into a Python thread complete with status information. The simplest way of doing this is to use:

```
PyGILState_STATE gstate= PyGILState_Ensure();
```

which creates the state struct and then acquires the GIL. To release the GIL use:

```
PyGILState_Release(gstate);
```

which releases both the GIL and the state struct.

To see this sort of approach in action we can run the Pi computation on two C threads, each computing half of the series. This needs us to split the original function into a function that does the computation and one that runs the threads.

For Windows, the computation is:

```
typedef struct
{
    int m;
    int n;
} range;

static int *Mutex;
static double PiShared = 0;

int PartPi(void *args)
{
    range *range1 = (range *)args;
    double pi, s;
    int m = range1->m;
    int n = range1->n;
    pi = 0;
```

```
    for (int k = m; k < n; k++)
      {
          s = 1;
          if (k % 2 == 0)
              s = -1;
          pi = pi + s / (2 * k - 1);
      }
      WaitForSingleObject(Mutex, INFINITE);
      PiShared += pi;
      ReleaseMutex(Mutex);
      return 0;
}
```

The change to passing a struct is needed to accommodate the way arguments are passed to a new thread. The Mutex is needed to allow a safe update of a shared variable. Each thread adds its contribution to the sum of the series to PiShared.

For Linux we have to use the standard POSIX threading system, Pthreads:

```
typedef struct
{
    int m;
    int n;
} range;

static int *Mutex;
static double PiShared = 0;

void *PartPi(void *args)
{
    range *range1 = (range *)args;
    double pi, s;
    int m = range1->m;
    int n = range1->n;
    pi = 0;
    for (int k = m; k < n; k++)
    {
        s = 1;
        if (k % 2 == 0)
            s = -1;
        pi = pi + s / (2 * k - 1);
    }
    pthread_mutex_lock(&mutex);
    PiShared += pi;
    pthread_mutex_unlock(&mutex);
    return NULL;
}
```

The only real difference is that we lock and unlock a mutex directly.

The function that runs the threads for Windows is:

```
static PyObject *Pi(PyObject *self, PyObject *args)
{
    int m, n;
    int *handles[2];

    if (!PyArg_ParseTuple(args, "ii", &m, &n))
        return NULL;

    Py_BEGIN_ALLOW_THREADS

    range range1 = {m, n / 2};
    range range2 = {n / 2 + 1, n};

    int threadId;
    Mutex = CreateMutex(NULL, FALSE, NULL);
    handles[0] = CreateThread(NULL, 0, PartPi, (void *)&range1,
                                                0, &threadId);
    handles[1] = CreateThread(NULL, 0, PartPi, (void *)&range2,
                                                0, &threadId);
    WaitForMultipleObjects(2, handles, TRUE, INFINITE);
    Py_END_ALLOW_THREADS
    return PyFloat_FromDouble(4 * PiShared);
}
```

It divides the range of the sum into two, creates two threads and gets them to compute each of the ranges. It then waits for both to finish and returns the shared variable with the total sum. Notice that the main thread releases the GIL but this has no effect on the two C threads as they can't acquire the GIL in their present form and indeed don't need to.

The Linux version again uses Pthreads and differs in only the way the threads are created and waited for:

```
static PyObject *Pi(PyObject *self, PyObject *args)
{
    int m, n;
    if (!PyArg_ParseTuple(args, "ii", &m, &n))
        return NULL;
    Py_BEGIN_ALLOW_THREADS
    range range1 = {m, n / 2};
    range range2 = {n / 2 + 1, n};
    int threadId;
    pthread_mutex_init(&mutex, NULL);
    pthread_t thread1, thread2;
    pthread_create(&thread1, NULL, PartPi, &range1);
    pthread_create(&thread2, NULL, PartPi, &range2);
    pthread_join(thread1,NULL);
    pthread_join(thread2,NULL);
    Py_END_ALLOW_THREADS
    return PyFloat_FromDouble(4 * PiShared);
}
```

The program runs in exactly the same way as the original Pi program and can also be used with Python threads:

```
import Pi
import time
import concurrent.futures
N=10000000
with concurrent.futures.ThreadPoolExecutor() as executor:

    t1=time.perf_counter()
    f1 = executor.submit(Pi.myPi,1,N)
    print("do some additional work")
    print("waiting for result")
    print(f1.result())
    t2=time.perf_counter()
    print((t2-t1)*1000)
```

Here the call to the submit returns at once and the call to result waits for the promise to resolve. On a machine with more than two cores available, this version runs a little faster than the single-threaded version. It completes in 30ms as opposed to 50ms, but not the 25ms that a simple-minded doubling of speed would suggest.

Acquiring The GIL

The two raw C threads do not interact with the Python C API. And so they do not need to acquire the GIL. As an example that does need the GIL, we can add an integer attribute to the module and let each of the threads in the PartPi function increment it. We need to modify the end of the PartPi function to read:

```
    PyGILState_STATE gstate = PyGILState_Ensure();
    PyObject *pimod = PyImport_AddModule("Pi");
    PyObject *myVal = PyObject_GetAttrString(pimod,"myValue");
    PyObject *myOne = PyLong_FromLong(1);
    PyObject *myInc = PyNumber_Add(myVal, myOne);
    int res= PyObject_SetAttrString((PyObject*)pimod,
                                    "myValue", myInc);
    PyGILState_Release(gstate);

    return 0;
}
```

First we get a reference to the Pi module. We could have passed this in when constructing the thread. Next we get the current value of myValue, add one to it and then send the result back as the new value of the attribute.

If you try this out you will find that the attribute is incremented by two as the two threads complete:

```python
import Pi
import time
import concurrent.futures
N=10000000
print("go")
with concurrent.futures.ThreadPoolExecutor() as executor:
    t1=time.perf_counter()
    f1 = executor.submit(Pi.myPi,1,N)
    print("do some additional work")
    print("waiting for result")
    r=f1.result()
    t2=time.perf_counter()
    print((t2-t1)*1000)
    print(r)
    print(Pi.myValue)
```

The final value of myValue is 44.

The complete listing for Linux:

```c
#define PY_SSIZE_T_CLEAN
#include <Python.h>

typedef struct
{
 int m;
 int n;
} range;

static pthread_mutex_t mutex;
static double PiShared = 0;

void *PartPi(void *args)
{
 range *range1 = (range *)args;
    double pi, s;
    int m = range1->m;
    int n = range1->n;
    pi = 0;
    for (int k = m; k < n; k++)
    {
        s = 1;
        if (k % 2 == 0)
            s = -1;
        pi = pi + s / (2 * k - 1);
    }
```

```
        pthread_mutex_lock(&mutex);
        PiShared += pi;
        pthread_mutex_unlock(&mutex);
        PyGILState_STATE gstate = PyGILState_Ensure();
        PyObject *pimod = PyImport_AddModule("Pi");
        PyObject *myVal = PyObject_GetAttrString(pimod, "myValue");
        PyObject *myOne = PyLong_FromLong(1);
        PyObject *myInc = PyNumber_Add(myVal, myOne);
        int res = PyObject_SetAttrString((PyObject *)pimod, "myValue",
                                                            myInc);
        PyGILState_Release(gstate);
        return NULL;
}
static PyObject *Pi(PyObject *self, PyObject *args)
{
        int m, n;
        if (!PyArg_ParseTuple(args, "ii", &m, &n))
            return NULL;
        Py_BEGIN_ALLOW_THREADS
        range range1 = {m, n / 2};
        range range2 = {n / 2 + 1, n};
        pthread_mutex_init(&mutex, NULL);
        pthread_t thread1, thread2;
        pthread_create(&thread1, NULL, PartPi, &range1);
        pthread_create(&thread2, NULL, PartPi, &range2);
        pthread_join(thread1, NULL);
        pthread_join(thread2, NULL);
        Py_END_ALLOW_THREADS
        return PyFloat_FromDouble(4 * PiShared);
}

static PyMethodDef AddMethods[] = {
    {"myPi", (PyCFunction)Pi, METH_VARARGS, "Compute Pi"},
    {NULL, NULL, 0, NULL} // sentinel
};

static struct PyModuleDef addmodule = {
    PyModuleDef_HEAD_INIT,
    "Pi",
    "C library to compute Pi",
    -1,
    AddMethods};

PyMODINIT_FUNC PyInit_Pi(void)
{
    PyObject *m = PyModule_Create(&addmodule);
    if (m == NULL)
        return NULL;
    PyObject *myValue = PyLong_FromLong(42);
    PyModule_AddObject(m, "myValue", myValue);
    return m;
}
```

The complete listing for Windows:

```c
#define PY_SSIZE_T_CLEAN
#include <Python.h>
#include <Windows.h>

typedef struct
{
    int m;
    int n;
} range;

static int *Mutex;
static double PiShared = 0;

int PartPi(void *args)
{
    range *range1 = (range *)args;
    double pi, s;
    int m = range1->m;
    int n = range1->n;
    pi = 0;
    for (int k = m; k < n; k++)
    {
        s = 1;
        if (k % 2 == 0)
            s = -1;
        pi = pi + s / (2 * k - 1);
    }
    WaitForSingleObject(Mutex, INFINITE);
    PiShared += pi;
    ReleaseMutex(Mutex);

    PyGILState_STATE gstate = PyGILState_Ensure();
    PyObject *pimod = PyImport_AddModule("Pi");
    PyObject *myVal = PyObject_GetAttrString(pimod, "myValue");
    PyObject *myOne = PyLong_FromLong(1);
    PyObject *myInc = PyNumber_Add(myVal, myOne);
    int res = PyObject_SetAttrString((PyObject *)pimod, "myValue",
                                                        myInc);

    PyGILState_Release(gstate);
    return 0;
}
```

```c
static PyObject *Pi(PyObject *self, PyObject *args)
{
    int m, n;
    int *handles[2];

    if (!PyArg_ParseTuple(args, "ii", &m, &n))
        return NULL;

    Py_BEGIN_ALLOW_THREADS

    range range1 = {m, n / 2};
    range range2 = {n / 2 + 1, n};

    int threadId;
    Mutex = CreateMutex(NULL, FALSE, NULL);
    handles[0] = CreateThread(NULL, 0, PartPi, (void *)&range1,
                                              0, &threadId);
    handles[1] = CreateThread(NULL, 0, PartPi, (void *)&range2,
                                              0, &threadId);

    WaitForMultipleObjects(2, handles, TRUE, INFINITE);
    Py_END_ALLOW_THREADS
    return PyFloat_FromDouble(4 * PiShared);
}

static PyMethodDef AddMethods[] = {
    {"myPi", (PyCFunction)Pi, METH_VARARGS, "Compute Pi"},
    {NULL, NULL, 0, NULL} // sentinel
};

static struct PyModuleDef addmodule = {
    PyModuleDef_HEAD_INIT,
    "Pi",
    "C library to compute Pi",
    -1,
    AddMethods};

PyMODINIT_FUNC PyInit_Pi(void)
{
    PyObject *m = PyModule_Create(&addmodule);
    if (m == NULL)
        return NULL;
    PyObject *myValue = PyLong_FromLong(42);
    PyModule_AddObject(m, "myValue", myValue);
    return m;
}
```

Callbacks

Callbacks are not a good way of handling asynchronous code, but they are easy for the consumer to understand and use. A better solution is to use a promise or `async` and `await`, but both of these are complex to implement via C. This means that for the C extension writer callbacks remain an attractive option. Arguably it would be better to ignore asynchronous operation in the C code and explain to the user how to implement an executor-based call so that a promise is automatically returned.

Implementing a callback isn't difficult, but it is slightly more involved than you might expect. The key is the function:

```
int Py_AddPendingCall(int (function, void *arg)
```

and the signature of the function is:

```
int function(void *arg)
```

Notice that this is a C function, not a Python function. It has no `PyObject` pointer as its first parameter and no tuple for arguments. What this means is that if we want to allow the user to set a Python callback we have to use the C callback to set up and call the Python function. The C function is added to a queue of pending functions which is processed one at a time when the Python interpreter is ready. The function is called by the main Python thread, which of course has the GIL. The function is called asynchronously with respect to the running Python code, but the interpreter will only call the function when it is on a bytecode boundary, i.e. it has completed an instruction and is about to start of the next and when it has the GIL. The C function has to return `0` if it is successful and `-1` with an exception otherwise.

The C function will not be interrupted by another pending function or by another Python thread unless it gives up the GIL. Notice that there is no guarantee that the C function will be called quickly. For example, if the Python interpreter is downloading something or executing a long running function it will be subject to delay.

To implement a Python callback we have to arrange for the `Pi` function to return as soon as possible and leave the computation to another function running on a new thread. This is fairly simple, but we need a struct to store the state of the computation to pass to the function that is doing the computation and then on to the callback when the computation is over. The subtle point, which often causes hours of wasted debugging, is that the struct that holds the state has to exist for the entire time that the computation is proceeding – you can't simply pass a local variable to the function running on the thread as it would be destroyed as soon as the `Pi` function returned. The simplest thing to do is allocate the object on the heap and free it when it is no longer needed. The new struct is:

```
typedef struct
{
    int m;
    int n;
    double Pi;
    PyObject *cb;
}State;
```

The fields m and n give the range of the sum, Pi is used to return the result and cb is the Python callback function.

The Windows Pi function is now;

```
static PyObject *Pi(PyObject *self, PyObject *args)
{
    int m, n;
    PyObject *cb;
    if (!PyArg_ParseTuple(args, "iiO:myPi", &m, &n, &cb))
        return NULL;
    State *state=(State*)malloc(sizeof(State));
    state->m = m;
    state->n = n;
    state->cb = cb;
    state->Pi = 0;
    int threadId;
    int *handle = CreateThread(NULL, 0, ComputePi, (void *)state,
                                                   0, &threadId);
    return PyLong_FromLong(0);
}
```

This starts ComputePi running on a new thread and then returns with a status of zero. Python calls the module function using:

```
Pi.myPi(1,N,myCallback)
```

where myCallback accepts a single parameter – the value of Pi.

```
def myCallback(pi):
    print("python callback")
    print(pi)
```

The Linux version just differs in thread creation:

```
    pthread_t thread1;
    pthread_create(&thread1, NULL, ComputePi,(void *) state);
```

Now we have to write `ComputePi` which has to accept the status struct, extract the information needed and then compute `Pi`:

```c
static int ComputePi(void *args)
{
    State *state = (State *)args;
    double pi, s;
    pi = 0;
    for (int k = state->m; k < state->n; k++)
    {
        s = 1;
        if (k % 2 == 0)
            s = -1;
        pi = pi + s / (2 * k - 1);
    }
    state->Pi = 4*pi;
    int res = Py_AddPendingCall(Ccb, (void *)state);
    return 0;
}
```

The value of m and n stored in `state` are used in the loop and the final answer, the value of Pi, is stored in the `state` before calling the C callback `Ccb` using the `AddPendingCall` function. The `Ccb` function has to use the information in `state` to call the Python function:

```c
int Ccb(void *args)
{
    State *state = (State *)args;
    printf("C callback called \n");
    PyObject *pi = Py_BuildValue("(f)",state->Pi);
    PyObject_CallObject((PyObject *)state->cb, pi);
    free(state);
    return 0;
}
```

As already mentioned, the thread running `Ccb` already has the GIL and so we can call API functions. In this case, the C double is converted to a Python float and then the Python function is called with it as a single argument. Notice that the C callback doesn't complete until the Python callback returns and this allows it to perform any cleanup operations to free the allocated memory for status. Adding error handling would complicate these functions a little, but you do need to make sure that there are no memory leaks due to an error.

A Python program to try this out is simple:

```python
import Pi
import time
def myCallback(pi):
    t2 = time.perf_counter()
    print((t2-t1)*1000)
    print("python callback")
    print(pi)

N = 10000000
t1 = time.perf_counter()
Pi.myPi(1,N,myCallback)
print("do some additional work")
while True:
    time.sleep(0.00001)
```

Using a callback adds around 5ms to the total time of 50ms. The final while loop is present to keep the program running if the callback takes a long time. There is currently a bug in Python 3.11 which means you have to put a call to sleep into the while loop to allow the main thread to call the pending function. It should just work with pass in the loop, but currently this only works if you run using debug.

The complete Windows program is:

```c
#define PY_SSIZE_T_CLEAN
#include <Python.h>
#include <Windows.h>

typedef struct
{
    int m;
    int n;
    double Pi;
    PyObject *cb;
}State;

int Ccb(void *args)
{
    State *state = (State *)args;
    printf("C callback called \n");
    PyObject *pi=Py_BuildValue("(f)",state->Pi);
    PyObject_CallObject((PyObject *)state->cb, pi);
    free(state);
    return 0;
}
```

```c
static int ComputePi(void *args)
{
    State *state = (State *)args;
    double pi, s;
    pi = 0;
    for (int k = state->m; k < state->n; k++)
    {
        s = 1;
        if (k % 2 == 0)
            s = -1;
        pi = pi + s / (2 * k - 1);
    }
    state->Pi=4*pi;
    int res = Py_AddPendingCall(Ccb, (void *)state);
    return 0;
}

static PyObject *Pi(PyObject *self, PyObject *args)
{
    int m, n;
    PyObject *cb;

    if (!PyArg_ParseTuple(args, "iiO:myPi", &m, &n, &cb))
        return NULL;
    State *state=(State*)malloc(sizeof(State));
    state->m = m;
    state->n = n;
    state->cb = cb;
    state->Pi = 0;
    int threadId;
    int *handle = CreateThread(NULL, 0, ComputePi, (void *)state,
                                                    0, &threadId);
    return PyLong_FromLong(0);
}

static PyMethodDef AddMethods[] = {
    {"myPi", (PyCFunction)Pi, METH_VARARGS, "Compute Pi"},
    {NULL, NULL, 0, NULL} // sentinel
};

static struct PyModuleDef addmodule = {
    PyModuleDef_HEAD_INIT,
    "Pi",
    "C library to compute Pi",
    -1,
    AddMethods};
```

```
PyMODINIT_FUNC PyInit_Pi(void)
{
    PyObject *m = PyModule_Create(&addmodule);
    if (m == NULL)
        return NULL;
    return m;
}
```

The Linux version differs only in the thread creation:

```
pthread_t thread1;
pthread_create(&thread1, NULL, ComputePi, (void *)state);
```

Summary

- The GIL makes the Python interpreter single-threaded. That is, only one thing can be happening in a Python program at any given time.

- Even if you write a C extension function which makes no use of threading, there is nothing stopping a Python programmer using it in a multi-threaded way.

- To make a C extension function non-blocking when used in a Python multi-threaded environment, you can release the GIL when not using Python objects or C API functions.

- You can also use C threads to speed up your functions, but only one thread can hold the GIL and hence work with the C API.

- A thread can acquire the GIL, but it might have to wait to do so.

- Callbacks are not a good way of getting results back to a Python program, but they are very simple to use from C.

Chapter 15

Embedding Python

So far we have only been considering extending Python by creating new modules which can be loaded into a Python program. A second approach to the problem is to embed the Python system within a C program. This is very similar to the task of extending Python and with a few small changes everything we have looked at so far applies to embedding Python.

Simple Embedding

The simplest way of embedding Python in a C program is to get it to execute a Python program without interacting with the C program. This isn't the usual way you want to do things, but it serves to get started. To load the Python interpreter you need to use:

```
Py_Initialize()
```

This loads and initializes the Python interpreter and all of the Python API functions. In principle, you should never use a Python C function before initialization, but there are exceptions.

When you are finished using Python you should unload it using:

```
Py_FinalizeEx()
```

There are many custom configurations that you can set to make the Python interpreter behave exactly as you want it. Most of these are obvious, if sometimes fiddly, and we will ignore them and concentrate on using the interpreter.

Once the interpreter is loaded, it just sits there waiting for you to give is some Python code to run. As well as the interpreter the entire Python runtime is loaded and this you can use via the C API without giving the interpreter some code to execute. This differs from the situation with an extension where the Python interpreter is loaded and starts running code which loads and uses your extension.

The simplest example of using the Python interpreter to run a Python program is:

```c
#define PY_SSIZE_T_CLEAN
#include <Python.h>

int main(int argc, char *argv[])
{
    Py_Initialize();
    PyRun_SimpleString("from time import time,ctime\n"
                       "print('Today is', ctime(time()))\n");
    Py_FinalizeEx();
  return 0;
}
```

The program simply loads the Python interpreter and then runs a small program which displays the current time and date. Notice that to run this program you need to compile it to an executable, not a shared library, and how this is achieved differs on Linux and Windows.

Embedding Under Windows

Under Windows, using VS Code and the Microsoft C compiler, the tasks.json file would be:

```json
{
    "tasks": [
        {
            "type": "cppbuild",
            "label": "C/C++: cl.exe build active file",
            "command": "cl.exe",
            "args": [
                "/Zi",
                "/EHsc",
                "/nologo",
                "/IC:/Users/user/AppData/Local/
                    Programs/Python/Python311/include",
                "/Fe${fileDirname}\\
                        ${fileBasenameNoExtension}.exe",
                "${file}",
                "/link /LIBPATH:C:/Users/user/AppData/
                        Local/Programs/Python/Python311/libs"
            ],
            "options": {
                "cwd": "${fileDirname}"
            },
            "problemMatcher": [
                "$msCompile"
            ],
```

```
    "group": {
            "kind": "build",
            "isDefault": true
        },
        "detail": "Task generated by Debugger."
    }
    ],
    "version": "2.0.0"
}
```

This is just the usual Task for building and running a .exe file. Debugging it also standard for an exe but, of course, you can't debug the Python code using a C debugger.

Embedding Under Linux

Linux is different from Windows in that the linker has to be told what shared libraries the executable wants to use. There is a utility, pythonx.y-config, that will tell you how to configure the compiler and linker. The x and y are the version numbers and the documentation says that it isn't guaranteed to work, but in practice it works for standard Linux. To find the linker flags required for embedding using Python3.11 you can use:

```
python3.11-config --ldflags --embed
```

which produces:

```
-L/usr/local/lib/python3.11/config-3.11-arm-linux-gnueabihf
  -L/usr/local/lib -lpython3.11 -lpthread -ldl  -lutil -lm
```

You can also use:

```
python3.11-config --cflags —embed
```

to find the compiler flags, but these are more a matter of personal preference and the standard flags work well.

The linker also needs to know about symbols in the libpythonx,y.so file and this needs the additional linker options:

```
-Xlinker -export-dynamic
```

Putting this together gives a basic `tasks.json` file:

```
{
    "tasks": [
        {
    "type": "cppbuild",
    "label": "C/C++: gcc-10 build active file",
    "command": "/usr/bin/gcc-10",
    "args": [
     "-fdiagnostics-color=always",
     "-g",
     "${file}",
     "-o",
     "${fileDirname}/${fileBasenameNoExtension}",
     "-I/usr/local/include/python3.11",
     "-L/usr/local/lib/python3.11/config-3.11-arm-linux-gnueabihf",
     "-L/usr/local/lib",
     "-Xlinker",
     "-export-dynamic",
                "-lpython3.11",
                "-lpthread",
                "-ldl",
                "-lutil",
                "-lm",

            ],
            "options": {
                "cwd": "${fileDirname}"
            },
            "problemMatcher": [
                "$gcc"
            ],
            "group": {
                "kind": "build",
                "isDefault": true
            },
            "detail": "Task generated by Debugger."
        }
    ],
    "version": "2.0.0"
}
```

With this modification you can run and debug an embedded program in the usual way.

Adding A Module

To interact with the interpreter you have to modify its configuration and the most usual way of doing this is to add a module, or more generally an object. You can create a module in the same way as always – the only difference is that you have to inform the interpreter that it exists before a program can import it.

For example, the function that computes Pi can be added in much the same way as for an extension:

```
#define PY_SSIZE_T_CLEAN
#include <Python.h>

static PyObject *Pi(PyObject *self, PyObject *args)
{
  int m, n;
  double pi, s;
  if (!PyArg_ParseTuple(args, "ii", &m, &n))
    return NULL;
  pi = 0;
  for (int k = m; k < n; k++)
  {
    s = 1;
    if (k % 2 == 0)
      s = -1;
    pi = pi + s / (2 * k - 1);
  }
  return PyFloat_FromDouble(4 * pi);
};

static PyMethodDef AddMethods[] = {
    {"myPi", Pi, METH_VARARGS, "Compute Pi"},
    {NULL, NULL, 0, NULL} // sentinel
};

static struct PyModuleDef addmodule = {
    PyModuleDef_HEAD_INIT,
    "Pi",
    "C library to compute Pi",
    -1,
    AddMethods};

PyMODINIT_FUNC PyInit_Pi(void)
{
  return PyModule_Create(&addmodule);
};
```

```
int main(int argc, char *argv[])
{

  PyImport_AppendInittab("Pi", &PyInit_Pi);
  Py_Initialize();
  PyRun_SimpleString("import Pi\n"
    "print(Pi.myPi(1,1000))\n");
  Py_FinalizeEx();
  return 0;
}
```

You can see that the only real difference is that we have to use the AppendInittab function to add the module to the list of built-in modules before we call PyInitialize. The program that is run still has to import the module before making use of it.

You can add any module in this way and make its attributes, including classes, available to the Python program that runs as part of the embedded system.

Python or C?

With Python embedded you have the choice of writing C to call Python functions or writing Python code to use the same functions behind the scenes. For example, we can call math.sqrt using API function or by running a Python program:

```
#define PY_SSIZE_T_CLEAN
#include <Python.h>

int main(int argc, char *argv[])
{
  Py_Initialize();
  PyObject *math =PyImport_ImportModule("math");
  PyObject *mathdict = PyModule_GetDict(math);
  PyObject *myFunction = PyDict_GetItemString(mathdict, "sqrt");
  PyObject *args = Py_BuildValue("(I)", 2);
  PyObject *result = PyObject_Call(myFunction, args, NULL);
  double res=PyFloat_AS_DOUBLE(result);
  printf("%f\n",res);

  PyRun_SimpleString(
    "import math\n"
    "print(math.sqrt(2))\n");

  Py_FinalizeEx();
  return 0;
}
```

If you run this you will see:

```
1.414214
1.4142135623730951
```

The first value comes from loading the math module, looking up sqrt in its dict and then calling the function. To display the result we convert to a C double. The second value comes from running the equivalent Python program.

Getting Results From Python

A common question is how to get a return value from a Python program. The simple answer is you can't. Python statements such as for, if and so on don't return results. Only a Python expression such as 2*2 or a function returns a result. You can evaluate an expression and get a return value using one of the PyRun_String functions.

For example:

```
PyObject* _g = PyDict_New();;
PyObject* _l = PyDict_New();
PyObject *pyResult= PyRun_String( "2+2",Py_eval_input, _g, _l);
int Cresult=PyLong_AS_LONG(pyResult);
printf("%d\n",Cresult);
```

The Py_eval_input makes PyRun_String evaluate an expression. The two dicts specify a global and local namespace of variables that can be used in the expression. For example, if we wanted to add X and Y:

```
PyObject* g = PyDict_New();
PyObject* l = PyDict_New();
PyDict_SetItemString(l,"X",PyLong_FromLong(2));
PyDict_SetItemString(l,"Y",PyLong_FromLong(2));
PyObject *pyResult= PyRun_String( "X+Y",Py_eval_input, g, l);
int Cresult=PyLong_AS_LONG(pyResult);
printf("%d\n",Cresult);
```

The main use of the global namespace is to allow the expression to use imported modules. For example to call math.sqrt you would use:

```
PyObject* g = PyDict_New();
PyObject* l = PyDict_New();
PyObject *math =PyImport_ImportModule("math");
PyDict_SetItemString(g, "math",math);
PyObject *pyResult= PyRun_String( "math.sqrt(2)",Py_eval_input, g,
l);
double res2=PyFloat_AS_DOUBLE(pyResult);
printf("%f\n",res2);
```

Notice that we have to load the math module and then make it available for the expression to use.

The full program can be seen on the book's webpage.

In a more general case, you can simply add a function that returns a result and runs it in the usual way, see the implementation of the Pi function at the start of the chapter.

Embedded Debugging

There is an advantage in using the embedded approach to developing Python extensions. You can debug your extension by simply running a C program in debug mode. There is no need to separately start a Python program and then attach a C debugger. You can simply allow the C program to load and run the Python interpreter. You can even load the Python program as a file and so make use of an IDE to write it. For example:

```c
#define PY_SSIZE_T_CLEAN
#include <Python.h>

static PyObject *Pi(PyObject *self, PyObject *args)
{
    int m, n;
    double pi, s;
    if (!PyArg_ParseTuple(args, "ii", &m, &n))
        return NULL;
    pi = 0;
    for (int k = m; k < n; k++)
    {
        s = 1;
        if (k % 2 == 0)
            s = -1;
        pi = pi + s / (2 * k - 1);
    }
    return PyFloat_FromDouble(4 * pi);
}

static PyMethodDef AddMethods[] = {
    {"myPi", Pi, METH_VARARGS, "Compute Pi"},
    {NULL, NULL, 0, NULL} // sentinel
};

static struct PyModuleDef addmodule = {
    PyModuleDef_HEAD_INIT,
    "Pi",
    "C library to compute Pi",
    -1,
    AddMethods};

PyMODINIT_FUNC PyInit_Pi(void)
{
    return PyModule_Create(&addmodule);
}
```

```
int main(int argc, char *argv[])
{

    PyImport_AppendInittab("Pi", &PyInit_Pi);
    Py_Initialize();
    PyObject *main = PyImport_AddModule("__main__");
    PyObject *mainDict = PyModule_GetDict(main);
    FILE *fp = fopen("Pi.py", "r");
    PyObject *l = PyDict_New();
    PyObject *result = PyRun_File(fp, "Pi.py",
                            Py_file_input, mainDict, l);

    Py_FinalizeEx();
    return 0;
}
```

Using this you can run and debug the `Pi.py` program saved on disk.

```
import Pi
import time
N=10000000
t1=time.perf_counter()
pi=Pi.myPi(1,N)
t2=time.perf_counter()
print((t2-t1)*1000)
print(pi)
```

At the time of writing, this program doesn't work under Windows due to a difficulty reading in the file using `PyRun_File`. A solution is to replace `PyRun_File` by:

```
char line[1000];
fread(line, 1, 1000, fp);
int res=PyRun_SimpleString(line);
```

Of course, the buffer has to be large enough to hold the entire file.

Implementing An Embedded API

If you plan to embed Python into an existing program then what you need to do is implement an API which gives the Python code access to the features you want to expose. You can proceed piecemeal and slowly add features, but it is much better to create an object hierarchy which encapsulates the features. Create a module which has objects that correspond to the data in the program and provide methods to access and process the data. A good example of an object hierarchy for embedded languages can be found in the scripting features of almost any spreadsheet.

Summary

- Embedding Python in a C program is closely related to writing a Python extension in C as the same C API functions are used.

- The key difference is that you have to initialize the Python interpreter before calling any C API functions.

- Once you have the interpreter initialized you can make use of it as if it had been invoked and initialized by running a Python program.

- You can add a modules to the system and so extend the Python interpreter when it is embedded.

- In an embedded system there is usually a choice of doing things in Python or in C and which is better depends on which is easier for the particular task.

- The only Python code that returns a result is an expression or a function. You can evaluate an expression using `PyRun_String`.

- Even if you are trying to develop an extension, it can be easier to debug it as an embedded system and load the Python program that makes use of the extension.

Index

257

Programmer's Python: Everything is an Object, Second Edition
ISBN: 978-1871962741

This is the first in the *Something Completely Different* series of book that look at what makes Python special and sets it apart from other programming languages. It explains the deeper logic in the approach that Python 3 takes to classes and objects. The subject is roughly speaking everything to do with the way Python implements objects - metaclass; class; object; attribute; and all of the other facilities such as functions, methods and the many "magic methods" that Python uses to make it all work.

Programmer's Python: Everything is Data
ISBN: 978-1871962595

Following the same philosophy, this book shows how Python treats data in a distinctly Pythonic way. Python's data objects are both very usable and very extensible. From the unlimited precision integers, referred to as bignums, through the choice of a list to play the role of the array, to the availability of the dictionary as a built-in data type, This book is what you need to help you make the most of these special features.

Programmer's Python: Async
ISBN: 978-1871962595

An application that doesn't make use of async code is wasting a huge amount of the machine's potential. Subtitled "Threads, processes, asyncio & more, this volume is about asynchronous programming, something that is is hard to get right, but well worth the trouble and reveals how Python tackles the problems in its own unique way.

Applying C For The IoT With Linux
ISBN: 978-1871962611

If you are using C to write low-level code using small Single Board Computers (SBCs) that run Linux, or if you do any coding in C that interacts with the hardware, this book brings together low-level, hardware-oriented and often hardware-specific information.

It starts by looking at how programs work with user-mode Linux. When working with hardware, arithmetic cannot be ignored, so separate chapters are devoted to integer, fixed-point and floating-point arithmetic. It goes on to the pseudo file system, memory-mapped files and sockets as a general-purpose way of communicating over networks and similar infrastructure. It continues by looking at multitasking, locking, using mutex and condition variables, and scheduling. Later chapters cover managing cores, and C11's atomics, memory models and barriers and it rounds out with a short look at how to mix assembler with C.

Fundamental C: Getting Closer To The Machine
ISBN: 978-1871962604

At an introductory level, this book explores C from the point of view of the low-level programmer and keeps close to the hardware.   It covers addresses, pointers, and how things are represented using binary and emphasizes the important idea is that everything is a bit pattern and what it means can change.

For beginners, the book covers installing an IDE and GCC before writing a Hello World program and then presents the fundamental building blocks of any program - variables, assignment and expressions, flow of control using conditionals and loops.

When programming in C you need to think about the way data is represented, and this book emphasizes the idea of modifying how a bit pattern is treated using type punning and unions and tackles the topic of undefined behavior, which is ignored in many books on C. A particular feature of the book is the way C code is illustrated by the assembly language it generates. This helps you understand why C is the way it is. And the way it was always intended to be written - close to the metal.

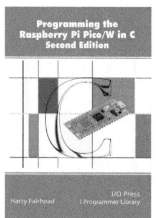

Programming The Raspberry Pi Pico/W In C, Second Edition
ISBN: 978-1871962796

The C version of this book explains the many reasons for wanting to use C with the Pico, not least of which is the fact that it is much faster. This makes it ideal for serious experimentation and delving into parts of the hardware that are otherwise inaccessible. Using C is the way to get the maximum from the Pico and to really understand how it works. The second edition covers the basics of using WiFi including web client and web server.

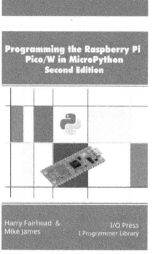

Programming the Raspberry Pi Pico/W in MicroPython Second Edition
ISBN: 978-1871962802

The MicroPython version of this book explains the many reasons for wanting to use Python with the Pico, not least the fact that it is easier to use. This makes it ideal for prototyping and education. It is slower than using C and programs use more memory, but sometimes this is a worthwhile trade off to get the sophistication of a higher-level language. What is surprising is how much you can do with Python plus I2C, SPI, PWM and PIO. The second edition covers the basics of using WiFi including web client and web server.

Master the Raspberry Pi Pico
ISBN: 978-1871962819

The extra capabilities added to the Pico W open up loads of opportunities, but only if you are prepared to do battle with the two libraries that provide networking and security – lwIP and mbedtls respectively. The problem with these large libraries of code is that they are poorly documented and don't refer directly to the Pico W and its SDK. This book sets out to remedy this by providing a guide to these libraries along with examples of what you can do with them.

Raspberry Pi IoT in C, Second Edition
ISBN: 978-1871962635

This book takes a practical approach to understanding electronic circuits and datasheets and translating this to code, specifically using the C programming language. The main reason for choosing C is speed, a crucial factor when you are writing programs to communicate with the outside world. If you are familiar with another programming language, C shouldn't be hard to pick up. This second edition has been brought up-to-date and focuses mainly on the Pi 4 and the Pi Zero.

The main idea in this book is to not simply install a driver, but to work directly with the hardware using the Raspberry Pi's GPIO (General Purpose Input Output) to connect with off-the-shelf sensors.

Raspberry Pi IoT in C With Linux Drivers
ISBN:9781871962642

There are Linux drivers for many off-the-shelf IoT devices and they provide a very easy-to-use, high-level way of working. The big problem is that there is very little documentation to help you get started. This book explains the principles so that you can tackle new devices and provides examples of using external hardware via standard Linux drivers with the Raspberry Pi 4 and Raspberry Pi Zero in the C language, which provides optimal performance.

Raspberry Pi IoT in Python With Linux Drivers
ISBN:9781871962659

If you opt to use Linux drivers to connect to external devices then Python becomes a good choice, as speed of execution is no longer a big issue. This book explains how to use Python to connect to and control external devices with the Raspberry Pi 4 and Raspberry Pi Zero using the standard Linux drivers.

www.ingramcontent.com/pod-product-compliance
Lightning Source LLC
LaVergne TN
LVHW062311060326
832902LV00013B/2156